The

Last Will and Testament

of

GEORGE WASHINGTON

and

Schedule of his Property

★ ★ ★

to which is appended

the

Last Will and Testament

of

MARTHA WASHINGTON

★

Edited by
JOHN C. FITZPATRICK

Introduction by
THE HONORABLE LEWIS F. POWELL, JR.

Published Through the Generosity of
FOLEY & LARDNER

BY THE MOUNT VERNON LADIES' ASSOCIATION
OF THE UNION

GEORGE WASHINGTON'S WATERMARK. The Wills of General and Mrs. Washington were both written on stationery specially made for Washington's use in 1792. The design was doubtless derived from a contemporary English paper showing Britannia in a similar pose.

Published by

THE MOUNT VERNON LADIES' ASSOCIATION
OF THE UNION

Copyright © 1939 by
The Mount Vernon Ladies' Association
of the Union
Mount Vernon, Virginia 22121
All rights reserved.
First Edition, 1939
Second Edition, 1947
Third Edition, 1960
Fourth Edition, 1972
Fifth Edition, 1982
Sixth Edition, revised, 1992
ISBN 0-931917-19-0
Printed in the United States of America

Library of Congress Cataloging-in-Publication Data

Washington, George, 1732-1799
   The last will and testament of George Washington and schedule of his property: to which is appended the last will and testament of Martha Washington / edited by John C. Fitzpatrick
      p.   cm.
   Includes index
   ISBN 0-931917-19-0
   1. Washington, George, 1732-1799 — Estate.   2. Washington, George, 1732-1799 — Will.   3. Washington, Martha, 1731-1802 — Estate.   4. Washington, Martha, 1731-1802 — Will   I. Washington, Martha, 1731-1802. II. Fitzpatrick, John Clement, 1876-1940.   III. Title. E312.99   1992
973.4'3'0922 — dc20   92-10576
                                                                                          CIP

CONTENTS

FOREWORD v

INTRODUCTION ix

THE LAST WILL AND TESTAMENT
    OF GEORGE WASHINGTON 1

NOTES TO THE WILL OF GEORGE WASHINGTON 30

SCHEDULE OF PROPERTY 41

NOTES TO THE SCHEDULE OF PROPERTY 50

THE LAST WILL AND TESTAMENT
    OF MARTHA WASHINGTON 55

NOTES TO THE WILL OF MARTHA WASHINGTON 62

FAMILY TREES 66

GENEALOGY 68

PERSONS MENTIONED IN THE WILLS 71

INDEX 75

COVER

George Washington, by Charles Willson Peale (1741-1827). Painted in September 1795, this classic portrait of Washington reflects the first president's strength and intelligence. Peale made the arrangements with Washington for a sitting at Philosophical Hall in Philadelphia, primarily to allow his son, seventeen year old Rembrandt Peale, to complete his first important commission. Before the day was over, five different members of the Peale family had created their own interpretations of Washington, giving rise to Gilbert Stuart's pun that Washington was being "Pealed all round."
(Courtesy of The New-York Historical Society, N.Y.C.)

BACK COVER

Washington's First Tomb, by William Thompson Russell Smith (1812-1896). A native of Scotland, Smith painted several different Mount Vernon scenes, including this peaceful rendition of Washington's original resting place. Almost forty years following Washington's death, after his remains were moved to a new tomb, the old tomb had deteriorated considerably. The door to the vault had been removed and the opening crudely blocked by boards. The path to the river was barricaded. Curiously, it appears that Smith began this work in 1836, set it aside for an unknown reason, and then finally finished the small painting more than fifty years later when he was in his eighties.
(The Mount Vernon Collections)

The New Tomb, artist unknown. "The family vault at Mount Vernon requiring repairs, and being improperly situated besides, I desire that a new one of brick, and upon a larger Scale, may be built at the foot of what is commonly called the Vineyard Inclosure. . . ." So wrote George Washington in his last will and testament. Although it took more than three decades, his nephew and executor Lawrence Lewis complied. By 1838, George and Martha Washington lay at rest in marble sarcophagi placed inside the vestibule. This undated view by an unknown artist is from the Marian S. Carson Collection, on loan to the Mount Vernon Ladies' Association.

FOREWORD

THE LAST WILL AND TESTAMENT OF GEORGE WASHINGTON was first printed for public distribution in Alexandria, Virginia, in the year 1800. Little attention was paid in that publication to the spelling, punctuation and manuscript peculiarities of the original and, though the Will has been published many times since 1800, few of these republications have been more scrupulously exact.

The first publication for distribution at Mount Vernon was made in 1868 by Mr. A. Jackson, of Washington, D.C., for whom the printing was done by Samuel Polkinhorn. This publisher's preface was dated at Fairfax Court House, Virginia, where the original Will was then, and is now, preserved.

The present publication by the Mount Vernon Ladies' Association of the Union follows the Jackson imprint, carefully corrected against a facsimile of the manuscript text of the original Will in Callahan's *Washington the Man and the Mason*, for spelling, punctuation and capitalization, disregarding only the manuscript line length which forms an unusual and impressive chirographic picture, but is exceedingly difficult to reproduce in type. In the manuscript the lines are carefully spaced and are of uniform length, dashes or waved strokes completing the lines where words would not quite fill out, and end-words are deliberately separated, without regard to their syllabic structure, to maintain an uniform right-hand margin. The note numbers are not, of course, in the original Will.

[v]

Washington's Will is twenty-eight and one-third pages long, on paper approximately 8½ x 6¾ inches in size. Written on both sides of the sheets and each page numbered by him, it is therefore a document of fifteen sheets and, being on his own specially made paper, bore his watermark in the center of each full-size sheet; these being quartered, to the mentioned size, bore in the corners quadrants of this water-mark. This special paper was first made for Washington in the 1790's; and the watermark is indicative of the man, as it was the draped figure of the goddess of agriculture, seated upon a plough, holding in one hand a staff surmounted with the Liberty Cap, and in the other a flowering twig; a broad band encircles the figure, within which is the name: GEORGE WASHINGTON; at the top of the band is a simplified version of the Washington crest, facing to the right.

Each of the twenty-nine pages of the Will, with one exception, is signed by Washington immediately below the center of the last line, but there is no means of knowing positively whether these signatures were written as each page was copied, or whether all were affixed at one time, after the entire Will was finished. The failure to sign page twenty-three is evidence either way, though the separation of words at the end of some of the pages rather militates against the probability of each page having been signed as finished. The last word on page twenty-three is the word "Washington" which may explain the omitted signature, as inducing the belief that the page had been signed. An almost identical inadvertency is found in the genealogical record, copied out by Washington for Sir Isaac Heard in 1792. There he writes that Augustine Washington (his father) "then married Ball", inadvertently omitting his mother's Christian name "Mary", undoubtedly from its close similarity in sound to the word "married" which preceded the name "Ball".

[vi]

There were two Wills existent when Washington was stricken with his fatal illness, and it is possible that one of these was the Will made in Philadelphia in the year 1775, just before the General started for Cambridge to take command of the Continental Army; but we have small grounds of surmise as to the provisions of the destroyed instrument or the date of its making. One of Lear's accounts of Washington's death relates that the General sent Mrs. Washington down to "his room" (the library) to get two Wills from his desk. He selected one, which he said was worthless and requested her to burn it, which she did; the other (the Will herewith) Mrs. Washington placed in her closet.

Washington died, Saturday night, December 14, 1799, between ten and eleven o'clock, and his Will was probated in the County Court of Fairfax, then holden in Alexandria, January 10, 1800. By a peculiar combination of circumstances the Will was thus probated within the boundaries of the seat of government of the Nation which George Washington had contributed so largely to create and found, Alexandria being then (and until the year 1801) in the District of Columbia and not in either Virginia or Fairfax County.

The Will, which is followed by the "Schedule of property" comprehended therein, is entirely in Washington's writing and was drawn up by him without legal aid of any kind. It is interesting in this connection to note that in Washington's youthful school exercises there is carefully copied out a "Form of a Short Will" with a note of the differences that should be incorporated in a will made in England and one made by an Englishman in France.

The Will has been in the custody of the Fairfax Clerk of the Court, with a few exceptions, since 1800. In 1861 at the outbreak of the Civil War, the document was folded

[vii]

vertically down the middle, placed in an envelope and taken to Richmond for safekeeping. The wisdom of this precaution was amply attested by what happened to the Will of Martha Washington which was left at the Fairfax Court House to be "liberated" by a Union soldier. (see Notes for Martha Washington's Will). Although George Washington's Will survived the war untouched, the paper suffered considerable damage where it weakened and tore along the fold. The first and second leaves of the Will became badly mutilated and the last leaf of Washington's "Notes" to the "Schedule of property" also lost many words of text. Several attempts were made to arrest the disintegration, including an effort to sew together the broken pages with a needle and thread. The Library of Congress undertook a major restoration of the document in 1910, using the best techniques of preservation of the time.

In 1977, by special act of the Virginia State Legislature, the Wills of George and Martha Washington were placed on loan for display at Mount Vernon for a period of six months. Following this exhibition, both of the Wills were again sent to the Library of Congress for further conservation work, before their return to the Fairfax County Court House.

INTRODUCTION

It is a privilege to participate in Mount Vernon's publication of a new edition of the Last Will and Testament of George Washington. This booklet provides both Americans and our guests from other countries with a unique opportunity to glimpse the character of the man our nation reveres above every other. Biographies of Washington literally number in the hundreds. His other papers, the product of a lifetime of methodical record keeping, fill 37 volumes. Yet the Last Will and Testament provides something not offered by any of these.

A will is a public document. Even for the ordinary man - and Washington was no ordinary man - a will is expected to be read by survivors and scrutinized by estate administrators. Yet a will is also intrinsically private. It usually provides for family and close friends, and may be used as a final statement of priorities and judgments that may not have found full expression in life. All this is true of George Washington's Will, which he entrusted to his wife Martha on his deathbed. It offers a unique window into the spirit that animated "the indispensable man."

Perhaps the most telling phrase found in Washington's Will is the first -- "I George Washington of Mount Vernon -- a citizen of the United States -- and lately President of the same . . . ." Washington identified himself not as a citizen of a state or a county, as was the custom of his day, but as a citizen of the United States. Above all else, Washington devoted himself to national unity, and to combating the twin ills of selfish local interest and entangling foreign influence.

One of Washington's bequests stands out from the others as a perfect symbol of his nationalism. In it, he wrote of his regret that the youth of the United States were so often sent to foreign countries for education, where they were likely to contract "not only habits of dissipation & extravagence, but principles unfriendly to Republican Governmt. and to the true & genuine liberties of mankind." To remedy this, Washington proposed a National University that would attract the brightest young students from all parts of the country. They would form nationwide friendships and learn principles of good government, "thereby to do away local attachments and State prejudices, as far as the nature of things would, or indeed ought to admit, from our National Councils."

Washington left 50 shares in the Potomac Company -- incorporated to promote another of Washington's unifying interests, inland navigation and commerce -- as an initial endowment for the National University. Washington hoped it would be established in the new District of Columbia, where he had only recently approved L'Enfant's city plan and laid the cornerstone of the Capitol. But even with the backing of Presidents Jefferson and Madison, the National University never came to be.

I am pleased to say that another of Washington's educational legacies has fared better. Along with the Potomac Company shares, Washington had been given 100 shares of the James River Company by the Virginia Legislature, which he resolved to put to public use. The James River Company shares were left to Liberty Hall Academy, a small school near the town of Lexington, Virginia. Liberty Hall later became Washington College, and then Washington and Lee University, my alma mater. Happily the James River shares were reinvested prior to the collapse of that company, and Washington's bequest remains a treasured part of the University's endowment.

Another prominent feature of Washington's Will reflects his personal effort to address the most shameful aspect of our nation's history, the institution of slavery. Second only to providing for his wife Martha, Washington's highest priority in the Will was his slaves. Especially after the Revolution, Washington had become increasingly troubled by the "peculiar institution." He favored the abolition of slavery by gradual measures, and wrote privately: "Not only do I pray for it, on the score of human dignity, I can clearly foresee that nothing but rooting out of slavery can perpetuate the existence of our Union."

Yet Washington was acutely aware that any public action on his part could produce political turmoil and imperil the national unity he strove to achieve. As biographer James Thomas Flexner has concluded, if Washington had been more audacious in his objections "he would undoubtedly have failed to achieve the end of slavery, and he would certainly have made impossible the role he played in the Constitutional Convention and the Presidency."

In his final testament, Washington no longer had to concern himself with public reaction. Moral duty, at last, compelled him to emancipate his slaves. Still, he faced practical obstacles. Washington did not own all of the slaves at Mount Vernon outright: about half were "dower" slaves restricted as to ownership by the will of Martha's first husband. The slaves of Mount Vernon had intermarried, and Washington recognized that to free half while the others remained bound could lead to untold grief. Washington therefore directed that the slaves be freed on Martha's death.

Realizing the hardships new freedom might entail, Washington directed that support be provided for slaves too young, old, or infirm to work. Washington sternly admonished his executors to respect his wishes for the care of the former slaves. He directed that the younger slaves be taught to read and write, and to pursue an occupation, though the law of the time prevented this from being carried out. Sadly, history shows that despite generous support from Washington's heirs, the freed slaves did not fare particularly well. In the end, slavery presented a practical morass in Washington's own affairs, just as it did for those of our nation. Nonetheless, Washington saw the Will as an opportunity to set a moral example in favor of freedom.

The details of the Will, no less than its grand themes, hold fascination for modern readers. Every aspect of the Will's preparation reflected Washington's meticulous attention. He compiled descriptions, locations, and estimates of value for the property he acquired during a lifetime of land speculation, and included these in the schedule of property attached to the Will. His holdings ranged from townhouse lots in Alexandria and the new Federal City, to the Great Dismal Swamp, to New York and Northwest Territory farmland. Washington's schedule even included investment advice for the future recipients of his property.

Less than two months before he wrote the Will in July 1799, Washington took a physical inventory of the livestock, land, and equipment on all five of the farms that made up the Mount Vernon estate. Mount Vernon was not only Washington's most prized possession and refuge, but also a community supporting hundreds of residents. In the words of biographer Douglas Southall Freeman, "What he wished to administer and perpetuate was more than mere investment in lands and houses, servants and time, crops and horses and equipment; it was investment in a way of living."

A will to accomplish this task deserved distinctive composition. Washington wrote on custom-made paper with a watermark depicting the goddess of agriculture holding a staff surmounted by a liberty cap. The entire Will is in Washington's own hand, and each page (save one inadvertent omission) is signed. Washington broke the words at the end of each line without regard to syllables, to form a straight right margin. The Will is, in short, a priceless national treasure that has retained great beauty despite the ravages of time.

Although Washington once advised a friend that "You will act very prudently in having your Will revised by some person skilled in the law," his own Will states that "no professional character" was consulted in its preparation. While he had no formal training in law, Washington did have experience as county court justice, land speculator, colonial legislator, and as an estate executor himself. This allowed him to pen a complex and sophisticated legal document that created life estates, divided vast holdings among numerous beneficiaries, and even provided for the contingency of lapse in the event a beneficiary died prior to receiving the inheritance.

In defense of the legal profession, I must add that Washington did enjoy the benefit of general advice on the Will from his attorney general, Edmund Randolph. And of course I cannot quarrel with Washington's appointment of his nephew Bushrod Washington, an associate justice of the Supreme Court, as an executor of the Will. Through the efforts of Martha and five other named executors, the vast estate was administered without resort to the surprisingly modern arbitration procedures Washington had included for the settlement of any disputes. The last tract finally sold no less than 52 years after Washington's death.

To reveal much more of the content of Washington's excellent composition would only diminish discoveries better made in the document itself. We find out, for example, who is to have the gold-headed walking cane given to Washington by Benjamin Franklin, who said that if the cane were a scepter, Washington would have deserved it. And Washington reveals the fate of "the Box made of the Oak that sheltered the Great Sir William Wallace after the battle of Falkirk," which was given to Washington with the instruction that he pass it on to the American who in Washington's view "should appear to merit it best."

In all its bequests, Washington's Will reveals both the private personality and the public spirit of its author. We need not only consider which relatives received his favorite swords, but also hear Washington's eloquent admonition with respect to their use in the defense of freedom. We are privileged to see not only Washington's personal expressions of admiration and devotion, but his broader vision of a prosperous America -- a republic free from slavery, where education is prized as the basis of enlightened democracy.

It is appropriate to conclude with a word about the Mount Vernon Ladies' Association of the Union. The Association's outstanding programs preserve the legacy of George Washington for future generations. They reflect unceasing devotion. This new edition of George Washington's Will is certain to shed new light on his character for a wider audience. In a day when Washington's values -- duty, patriotism, family loyalty, modesty, and selflessness in public service -- are so sorely needed, the Association's work has never been more important.

Justice Lewis F. Powell, Jr.
Retired
Supreme Court of the United States

The
Last Will and Testament
of
GEORGE WASHINGTON

In the name of God amen

I George Washington of Mount Vernon—a citizen of the United States,—and lately President of the same, do make, ordain and declare this Instrument; which is written with my own hand and every page thereof subscribed with my name, to be my last Will & Testament, revoking all others.

Imprimus.   All my debts, of which there are but few, and none of magnitude, are to be punctually and speedily paid—and the Legacies hereinafter bequeathed, are to be discharged as soon as circumstances will permit, and in the manner directed—

Item.   To my dearly beloved wife Martha Washington[1] I give and bequeath the use, profit and benefit of my whole Estate,[2] real and personal, for the term of her natural life—except such parts thereof as are specifically disposed of hereafter:—My improved lot in the Town of Alexandria, situated on Pitt & Cameron Streets,[3] I give to her and her heirs forever, as I also do my

G:o Washington

[1]

household & Kitchen furniture of every sort & kind, with the liquors and groceries which may be on hand at the time of my decease; to be used & disposed of as she may think proper.

Item   Upon the decease of my wife, it is my Will & desire that all the Slaves which I hold in *my own right*, shall receive their freedom.—To emancipate them during her life, would, tho' earnestly wished by me, be attended with such insuperable difficulties on account of their intermixture by Marriages with the Dower Negroes,[4] as to excite the most painful sensations, if not disagreeable consequences from the latter, while both descriptions are in the occupancy of the same Proprietor; it not being in my power, under the tenure by which the Dower Negros are held, to manumit them.—And whereas among those who will receive freedom according to this devise, there may be some, who from old age or bodily infirmities, and others who on account of their infancy, that will be unable to support themselves; it is my Will and desire that all who come under the first & second description shall be comfortably cloathed & fed by my heirs while they live;—and

G Washington

that such of the latter descripton as have no parents living, or if living are unable, or unwilling to provide for them, shall be bound by the Court until they shall arrive at the age of twenty five years;—and in cases where no record can be produced, whereby their ages can be ascertained, the judgment of the Court upon its own view of the subject, shall be adequate and final.—The Negros thus bound, are (by their Masters or Mistresses) to be taught to read & write; and to be brought up to some useful occupation, agreeably to the Laws of the Commonwealth of Virginia, providing for the support of Orphan and other poor Children.—And I do hereby expressly forbid the Sale, or transportation out of the said Commonwealth, of any Slave I may die possessed of, under any pretence whatsoever.—And I do moreover most pointedly, and most solemnly enjoin it upon my Executors hereafter named, or the Survivors of them, to see that *this* clause respecting Slaves, and every part thereof be religiously fulfilled at the Epoch at which it is directed to take place; without evasion, neglect or delay, after the Crops which may then be on the ground are harvested, particularly as it respects

[3]

the aged and infirm;—Seeing that a regular and permanent fund be established for their Support so long as there are subjects requiring it; not trusting to the uncertain provision to be made by individuals.⁵— And to my Mulatto man William (calling himself William Lee)⁶ I give immediate freedom; or if he should prefer it (on account of the accidents which have befallen him, and which have rendered him incapable of walking or of any active employment) to remain in the situation he now is, it shall be optional in him to do so: In either case however, I allow him an annuity of thirty dollars during his natural life, which shall be independent of the victuals and cloaths he has been accustomed to receive, if he chuses the last alternative; but in full, with his freedom, if he prefers the first;—& this I give him as a testimony of my sense of his attachment to me, and for his faithful services during the Revolutionary War.—

Item   To the Trustees (Governors, or by whatsoever other name they may be designated) of the Academy in the Town of Alexandria,⁷ I give and bequeath, in Trust, four thousand dollars, or in other words twenty of the shares which I

[4]

hold in the Bank of Alexandria, towards the support of a Free school established at, and annexed to, the said Academy; for the purpose of Educating such Orphan children, or the children of such other poor and indigent persons as are unable to accomplish it with their own means; and who, in the judgment of the Trustees of the said Seminary, are best entitled to the benefit of this donation.—The aforesaid twenty shares I give & bequeath in perpetuity;—the dividends only of which are to be drawn for, and applied by the said Trustees for the time being, for the uses above mentioned;—the stock to remain entire and untouched; unless indications of a failure of the said Bank should be so apparent, or a discontinuance thereof should render a removal of this fund necessary;—in either of these cases, the amount of the Stock here devised, is to be vested in some other Bank or public Institution, whereby the interest may with regularity & certainby[8] be drawn, and applied as above.—And to prevent misconception, my meaning is, and is hereby declared to be that these twenty shares are in lieu of, and not in addition to, the thousand pounds given by a missive letter[9] some years ago; in consequence whereof an an=

nuity of fifty pounds has since been paid towards the support of this Institution.

Item   Whereas by a Law of the Commonwealth of Virginia, enacted in the year 1785, the Legislature thereof was pleased (as a an evidence of Its approbation of the services I had rendered the Public during the Revolution—and partly, I believe, in consideration of my having suggested the vast advantages which the Community would derive from the extension of its Inland Navigation, under Legislative patronage) to present me with one hundred shares of one hundred dollars each, in the incorporated company established for the purpose of extending the navigation of James River from tide water to the Mountains: and also with fifty shares of one hundred pounds Sterling each, in the Corporation of another company, likewise established for the similar purpose of opening the Navigation of the River Potomac from tide water to Fort Cumberland;[10] the acceptance of which, although the offer was highly honourable, and grateful to my feelings, was refused, as inconsistent with a principle which I had adop

[6]

ted, and had never departed from—namely—not to receive pecuniary compensation for any services I could render my country in its arduous struggle with great Britain, for its Rights; and because I had evaded similar propositions from other States in the Union; —adding to this refusal, however, an intimation that, if it should be the pleasure of the Legislature to permit me to appropriate the said shares to *public uses*, I would receive them on those terms with due sensibility;—and this it having consented to, in flattering terms, as will appear by a subsequent Law, and sundry resolutions, in the most ample and honourable manner, I proceed after this recital, for the more correct understanding of the case, to declare—

That as it has always been a source of serious regret with me, to see the youth of these United States sent to foreign Countries for the purpose of Education, often before their minds were formed, or they had imbibed any adequate ideas of the happiness of their own;—contracting, too frequently, not only habits of dissipation & extravagence, but principles unfriendly to Republican Governmt. and to the true & genuine liberties

of mankind; which, thereafter are rarely overcome.—
For these reasons, it has been my ardent wish to see a
plan devised on a liberal scale which would have a
tendency to sprd. systemactic ideas through all parts
of this rising Empire, thereby to do away local
attachments and State prejudices, as far as the nature
of things would, or indeed ought to admit, from our
National Councils.—Looking anxiously forward to
the accomplishment of so desirable an object as this
is (in my estimation) my mind has not been able to
contemplate any plan more likely to effect the
measure than the establishment of a UNIVERSITY[11]
in a central part of the United States, to which the
youth of fortune and talents from all parts thereof
might be sent for the completion of their Education
in all the branches of polite literature;—in arts and
Sciences,—in acquiring knowledge in the principles
of Politics and good Government;—and (as a matter
of infinite Importance in my judgment) by associat-
ing with each other, and forming friendships in
Juvenile years, be enabled to free themselves in a
proper degree from those local prejudices and habi=

tual jealousies which have just been mentioned; and which, when carried to excess, are never failing sources of disquietude to the Public mind, and pregnant of mischievous consequences to this Country:—Under these impressions, so fully dilated,

Item   I give and bequeath in perpetuity the fifty shares which I hold in the Potomac Company (under the aforesaid Acts of the Legislature of Virginia) towards the endowment of a UNIVERSITY to be established within the limits of the District of Columbia, under the auspices of the General Government, if that government should incline to extend a fostering hand towards it;—and until such Seminary is established, and the funds arising on these shares shall be required for its support, my further Will & desire is that the profit accruing therefrom shall, whenever the dividends are made, be laid out in purchasing Stock in the Bank of Columbia, or some other Bank, at the discretion of my Executors; or by the Treasurer of the United States for the time being under the direction of Congress; provided that Honourable body should

[9]

Patronize the measure, and the Dividends proceeding from the purchase of such Stock is to be vested in more stock, and so on, until a sum adequate to the accomplishment of the object is obtained, of which I have not the smallest doubt, before many years passes away; even if no aid or encouraged is given by Legislative authority, or from any other source

Item   The hundred shares which I held in the James River Company, I have given, and now confirm in perpetuity to, and for the use & benefit of Liberty-Hall Academy,[12] in the County of Rockbridge, in the Commonwealth of Virga.

Item   I release exonerate and discharge, the Estate of my deceased brother Samuel Washington, from the payment of the money which is due to me for the Land I sold to Philip Pendleton (lying in the County of Berkeley) who assigned the same to him the said Samuel; who, by agreement was to pay me therefor.—And whereas by some contract (the purport of which was never communicated to me) between the said Samuel and his son Thornton Washington, the latter became possessed of the aforesaid Land, without

G:Washington

any conveyance having passed from me, either to the said Pendleton, the said Samuel, or the said Thornton, and without any consideration having been made, by which neglect neither the legal nor equitable title has been alienated;—it rests therefore with me to declare my intentions concerning the Premises —and these are, to give & bequeath the said land to whomsoever the said Thornton Washington (who is also dead) devised the same; or to his heirs forever if he died Intestate:—Exonorating the estate of the said Thornton, equally with that of the said Samuel from payment of the purchase money; which, with Interest; agreeably to the original contract with the said Pendleton, would amount to more than a thousand pounds.—And whereas two other Sons of my said deceased brother Samuel—namely, George Steptoe Washington and Lawrence Augustine Washington, were, by the decease of those to whose care they were committed, brought under my protection, and in conseqe. have occasioned advances on my part for their Education[13] at College, and other Schools, for their board—cloathing—and other incidental expences, to the amount of near

five thousand dollars over and above the Sums furnished by their Estate wch—Sum may be inconvenient for them, or their fathers Estate to refund. I do for these reasons acquit them, and the said estate, from the payment thereof.—My intention being, that all accounts between them and me, and their fathers estate and me shall stand balanced.—

Item   The balance due to me from the Estate of Bartholomew Dandridge deceased (my wife's brother) and which amounted on the first day of October 1795 to four hundred and twenty five pounds (as will appear by an account rendered by his deceased son John Dandridge, who was the acting Exr. of his fathers Will) I release & acquit from the payment thereof.—And the Negros, then thirty three in number) formerly belonging to the said estate, who were taken in execution—sold—and purchased in on my account in the year   and ever since have remained in the possession, and to the use of Mary, Widow of the said Bartholomew Dandridge, with their increase, it is my Will & desire shall continue, & be in her possession, without paying hire, or ma

G:Washington

king compensation for the same for the time past or to come, during her natural life; at the expiration of which, I direct that all of them who are forty years old & upwards, shall receive their freedom; all under that age and above sixteen, shall serve seven years and no longer; and all under sixteen years, shall serve until they are twenty five years of age, and then be free.—And to avoid disputes respecting the ages of any of these Negros, they are to be taken to the Court of the County in which they reside, and the judgment thereof, in this relation shall be final; and a record thereof made; which may be adduced as evidence at any time thereafter, if disputes should arise concerning the same.—And I further direct, that the heirs of the said Bartholomew Dandridge shall, equally, share the benefits arising from the Services of the said negros according to the tenor of this devise, upon the decease of their Mother.

Item   If Charles Carter who intermarried with my niece Betty Lewis[14] is not sufficiently secured in the title to the lots he had of me in the Town of Fredericksburgh, it is my Will & desire that my Executors shall make such conveyances of them as the Law requires, to render it perfect.—

Item   To my Nephew William Augustine Washing-ton[15] and his heirs (if he should conceive them to be objects worth prosecuting) and to his heirs,[16]—a lot in the Town of Manchester (opposite to Richmond) No 265 drawn on my sole account, and also the tenth of one or two, hundred acre lots, and two or three half acre lots in the City, and vicinity of Richmond, drawn in partnership with nine others, all in the lottery of the deceased William Byrd[17] are given—as is also a lot which I purchased of John Hood, conveyed by William Willie and Samuel Gordon Trustees of the said John Hood, numbered 139 in the Town of Edinburgh, in the County of Prince George, State of Virginia

Item   To my Nephew Bushrod Washington,[18] I give and bequeath all the Papers in my possession, which relate to my Civel and Military Administration of the affairs of this Country;—I leave to him also, such of my private Papers as are worth preserving;—and at the decease of wife, and before—if she is not inclined to retain them, I give and bequeath my library of Books, and Pamphlets of every kind.—

Item   Having sold Lands which I possessed in the State of Pennsylvania, and part of a tract held in equal right with George Clinton, late Governor of New York, in the State of New York;—my share of land, & interest, in the Great Dismal Swamp,[19] and a tract of land which I owned in the County of Gloucester;[20]—withholding the legal titles thereto, until the consideration money should be paid.—And having moreover leased, & conditionally sold (as will appear by the tenor of the said leases) all my lands upon the Great Kanhawa,[21] and a tract upon Difficult Run,[22] in the county of Loudoun, it is my Will and direction, that whensoever the Contracts are fully, & respectively complied with, according to the spirit, true intent & meaning thereof, on the part of the purchasers, their heirs or Assigns, that then, and in that case, Conveyances are to be made, agreeably to the terms of the said Contracts; and the money arising therefrom, when paid, to be vested in Bank stock; the dividends whereof, as of that also wch—is already vested therein, is to inure to my said Wife during her life—but the Stock itself is to remain, &

be subject to the general distribution hereafter directed.

Item To the Earl of Buchan I recommit "the Box made of the Oak that sheltered the Great Sir William Wallace after the battle of Falkirk"[23] presented to me by his Lordship, in terms too flattering for me to repeat,—with a request "to pass it, on the event of my decease, to the man in my country, who should appear to merit it best, upon the same conditions that have induced him to send it to me." Whether easy, or not, to select *the man* who might comport with his Lordships opinion in this respect, is not for me to say; but conceiving that no disposition of this valuable curiosity can be more eligable than the re-commitment of it to his own Cabinet, agreeably to the original design of the Goldsmiths Company of Edenburgh, who presented it to him, and at his request, consented that it should be transfered to me; I do give & bequeath the same to his Lordship, and in case of his decease, to his heir with my grateful thanks for the distinguished honour of presenting it to me; and more especially for the favourable sentiments

G:Washington

with which he accompanied it.

Item   To my brother Charles Washington I give &
bequeath the gold headed Cane left me by Doctr.
Franklin in his Will.[24]—I add nothing to it, because of
the ample provision I have made for his Issue.—To
the acquaintances and friends of my Juvenile years,
Lawrence Washington & Robert Washington of
Chotanck,[25] I give my other two gold headed Canes,
having my Arms engraved on them; and to each (as
they will be useful where they live) I leave one of the
Spy-glasses which constituted part of my equipage
during the late War.—To my compatriot in arms, and
old & intimate friend Doctr. Craik,[26] I give my
bureau (or as the Cabinet makers call it, Tambour
Secretary) and the circular chair—an appendage of
my Study.—To Doctor David Stuart[27] I give my large
shaving & dressing Table, and my Telescope.—To
the Reverend, now Bryan, Lord Fairfax,[28] I give a
Bible in three large folio volumes, with notes, presented to me by the Right reverend Thomas Wilson,
Bishop of Sodor & Man.—To General de la Fayette[29]
I give a pair of finely wrought steel Pistols, taken
from the enemy in the Revolutionary War.—To my
Sisters in law

Hannah Washington & Mildred Washington,—to my friends Eleanor Stuart, Hannah Washington of Fairfield, and Elizabeth Washington of Hayfield,[30] I give, each, a mourning Ring of the value of one hundred dollars.—These bequests are not made for the intrinsic value of them, but as mementos of my esteem & regard.—To Tobias Lear,[31] I give the use of the Farm which he now holds, in virtue of a Lease from me to him and his deceased wife (for and during their natural lives) free from Rent, during his life;—at the expiration of which, it is to be disposed as is hereinafter directed.—To Sally B. Haynie[32] (a distant relation of mine) I give and bequeath three hundred dollars—To Sarah Green daughter of the deceased Thomas Bishop, and to Ann Walker daughter of Jno. Alton,[33] also deceased, I give, each one hundred dollars, in consideration of the attachment of their fathers to me, each of whom having lived nearly forty years in my family.—To each of my Nephews, William Augustine Washington, George Lewis, George Steptoe Washington, Bushrod Washington and Samuel Washington, I give one of the Swords or Cutteaux of which I may die pos

sessed;[34] and they are to chuse in the order they are named.—These Swords are accompanied with an injunction not to unsheath them for the purpose of shedding blood, except it be for self defence, or in defence of their Country and its rights; and in the latter case, to keep them unsheathed, and prefer falling with them in their hands, to the relinquishment thereof

And now

Having gone through these specific devises, with explanations for the more correct understanding of the meaning and design of them; I proceed to the distribution of the more important parts of my Estate, in manner following—

First   To My Nephew Bushrod Washington and his heirs (partly in consideration of an intimation to his deceased father[35] while we were Bachelors, & he had kindly undertaken to superintend my Estate during my Military Services in the former War between Great Britain & France, that if I should fall therein, Mount Vernon[36] (then less extensive in domain than at present) should become his property) I give and bequeath all that part thereof which is comprehen

ded within the following limits—viz—Beginning at the ford of Dogue run, near my Mill, and extending along the road, and bounded thereby as it now goes, & ever had gone since my recollection of it, to the ford of little hunting Creek at the Gum spring until it comes to a knowl, opposite to an old road which formerly passed through the lower field of Muddy hole Farm; at which, on the north side of the said road are three red, or Spanish Oaks marked as a corner, and a stone placed.—thence by a line of trees to be marked, rectangular to the back line, or outer boundary of the tract between Thomson Mason[37] & myself.—thence with that line Easterly (now double ditching with a Post & Rail fence thereon) to the run of little hunting Creek.—thence with that run which is the boundary between the Lands of the late Humphrey Peake[38] and me, to the tide water of the said Creek; thence by that water to Potomac River.— thence with the River to the mouth of Dogue Creek. —and thence with the said Dogue Creek to the place of beginning at the aforesaid ford; containing upwards of four thousand Acres, be the same more or less—together with the Mansion house

and all other buildings and improvemts. thereon.

Second   In consideration of the consanguinity between them and my wife, being as nearly related to
her as to myself, as on account of the affection I had
for, and the obligation I was under to, their father
when living, who from his youth had attached
himself to my person, and followed my fortunes
through the viscissitudes of the late Revolution[39]—
afterwards devoting his time to the Superintendence
of my private concerns for many years, whilst my
public employments rendered it impracticable for me
to do it myself, thereby affording me essential
Services, and always performing them in a manner
the most felial and respectful—for these reasons I
say, I give and bequeath to George Fayette Washington, and Lawrence Augustine Washington and their
heirs, my Estate East of little hunting Creek,—lying
on the River Potomac;—including the Farm of 360
Acres, Leased to Tobias Lear as noticed before, and
containing in the whole, by Deeds, Two thousand
and Seventy seven acres—be it more or less.—Which
said Estate it is my Will and desire should be
equitably, & advantageously divided between them,
according to quantity, quality & other circumstances
when

the youngest shall have arrived at the age of twenty one years, by three judicious and disinterested men; —one to be chosen by each of the brothers, and the third by these two.—In the meantime, if the termination of my wife's interest therein should have ceased, the profits arising therefrom are to be applied for their joint uses and benefit.

Third   And whereas it has always been my intention, since my expectation of having Issue has ceased, to consider the Grand children of my wife in the same light as I do my own relations, and to act a friendly part by them; more especially by the two whom we have reared from their earliest infancy—namely— Eleanor Parke Custis, & George Washington Parke Custis.[40] And whereas the former of these hath lately intermarried with Lawrence Lewis, a son of my deceased Sister Betty Lewis, by which union the inducement to provide for them both has been increased;—Wherefore, I give & bequeath to the said Lawrence Lewis & Eleanor Parke Lewis, his wife, and their heirs, the residue of my Mount Vernon Estate, not already devised to my Nephew Bushrod Washington,—comprehended within the following description.[41]—viz—All the land North of the Road leading from the ford of Dogue run to the Gum spring as described in the devise of the other part of the tract, to Bushrod Washington, until it comes to the Stone & three red or Spanish Oaks on the knowl.—thence with the rectangular line to the back line (between Mr. Mason & me)—thence with that line westerly, along the new double ditch to Dogue run, by the tumbling Dam of my Mill;— thence with the said run to the ford aforementioned; —to which I add all the Land I possess West of the said Dogue run, & Dogue Crk—bounded Easterly & Southerly thereby;—together with the Mill, Distill-ery,[42] and all other houses & improvements on the premises, making together about two thousand Acres—be it more or less.

Fourth   Actuated by the principal already mentioned, I give and bequeath to George Washington Parke Curtis, the Grandson of my wife, and my Ward, and to his heirs, the tract I hold on four mile run[43] in the vicinity of Alexandria, containing one thousd—two hundred acres, more or less,—& my entire Square, number twenty one, in the City of Washington.[44]

Fifth   All the rest and residue of my Estate, real &
personal—not disposed of in manner aforesaid—In
whatsoever consisting—wheresoever lying—and
whensoever found—a schedule of which, as far as is
recollected, with a reasonable estimate of its value, is
hereunto annexed—I desire may be sold by my
Executors at such times—in such manner—and on
such credits (if an equal, valid, and satisfactory
distribution of the specific property cannot be made
without)—as, in their judgment shall be most condu-
cive to the interest of the parties concerned; and the
monies arising therefrom to be divided into twenty
three equal parts,[45] and applied as follow—viz—

To William Augustine Washington, Elizabeth
Spotswood, Jane Thornton, and the heirs of Ann
Ashton; son, and daughters of my deceased brother
Augustine Washington,[46] I give and bequeath four
parts;—that is—one part to each of them.

To Fielding Lewis, George Lewis, Robert Lewis,
Howell Lewis & Betty Carter, sons and daughter of
my deceased Sister Betty Lewis, I give & bequeath
five other parts—one to each of them

To George Steptoe Washington, Lawrence Augustine Washington, Harriot[47]

[24]

Parks, and the heirs of Thornton Washington, sons and daughter of my deceased brother Samuel Washington, I give and bequeath other four parts, one part to each of them.

To Corbin Washington, and the heirs of Jane Washington,[48] Son & daughter of my deceased Brother John Augustine Washington, I give & bequeath two parts;—one part to each of them.

To Samuel Washington, Francis Ball & Mildred Hammond,[49] son and daughters of my Brother Charles Washington, I give & bequeath three parts;—one part to each of them.—And to George Fayette Washington Charles Augustine Washington & Maria Washington,[50] sons and daughter of my deceased Nephew Geo: Augustine Washington, I give one other part;—that is—to each a third of that part.

To Elizabeth Parke Law, Martha Parke Peter, and Eleanor Parke Lewis,[51] I give and bequeath three other parts,—that is a part to each of them.

And to my Nephews Bushrod Washington & Lawrence Lewis,—and to my ward,[52] the grandson of My wife, I give and bequeath one other part;—that is, a third thereof to each of them.—And if it should so happen, that any of the persons whose names are here ennumerated (unknown to me) should now

be deceased—or should die before me, that in either of these cases, the heirs of such deceased person shall, notwithstanding, derive all the benefits of the bequest; in the same manner as if he, or she, was actually living at the time.

And by way of advice, I recommend it to my Executors not to be precipitate in disposing of the landed property (herein directed to be sold) if from temporary causes the Sale thereof should be dull; experience having fully evinced, that the price of land (especially above the Falls of the Rivers, & on the Western Waters) have been progressively rising, and cannot be long checked in its increasing value.—And I particularly recommend it to such of the Legatees (under this clause of my Will) as can make it convenient, to take each a share of my Stock in the Potomac Company in preference to the amount of what it might sell for; being thoroughly convinced myself, that no uses to which the money can be applied will be so productive as the Tolls arising from this navigation when in full operation (and this from the nature of things it must be 'ere long) and more especially if that of the Shanondoah is added thereto.[53]

The family Vault at Mount Vernon requiring repairs, and being improperly situated besides, I desire that a new one of Brick, and upon a larger Scale, may be built at the foot of what is commonly called the Vineyard Inclosure,—on the ground which is marked out.[54]—In which my remains with those of my deceased relatives (now in the old Vault) and such others of my family as may chuse to be entombed there, may be deposited.—And it is my express desire that my Corpse may be Interred in a private manner, without—parade, or funeral Oration.[55]

Lastly I constitute and appoint my dearly beloved wife Martha Washington, My Nephews William Augustine Washington, Bushrod Washington, George Steptoe Washington, Samuel Washington, & Lawrence Lewis, & my ward George Washington Parke Custis (when he shall have arrived at the age of twenty years) Executrix & Executors of this Will & testament,—In the construction of which it will readily be perceived that no professional character has been consulted, or has had any Agency in the draught—and that, although it has occupied many of my leisure hours to digest, & to through[56] it into its present form, it may, notwithstanding, appear crude and incorrect.—But having endeavoured to be plain, and explicit in all the Devises—even at the expence of prolixity, perhaps of tautology, I hope, and trust, that no disputes will arise concerning them; but if, contrary to expectation, the case should be otherwise from the want of legal expression, or the usual technical terms, or because too much or too little has been said on any of the Devises to be consonant with law, My Will and direction expressly is, that all disputes (if unhappily any should arise) shall be decided by three impartial and intelligent men, known for their probity and good understanding; two to be chosen by the disputants—each having the choice of one—and the third by those two. Which three men thus chosen, shall, unfettered by Law, or legal constructions, declare their Sense of the Testators intention;—and such decision is, to all intents and purposes to be as binding on the Parties as if it had been given in the Supreme Court of the United States.[57]

In witness of all, and of each of the things herein contained, I have set my hand and Seal, this ninth day of July, in the year One thousand seven hundred and ninety[38] and of the Independence of the United States the twenty fourth.

G. Washington (Seal)

NOTES FOR
GEORGE WASHINGTON'S WILL

[1] Martha Dandridge Custis Washington, daughter of Colonel John Dandridge, of New Kent County, Virginia, and widow of Daniel Parke Custis.

[2] The Mount Vernon property emerged for the first time as a distinct area in the original grant from Lord Culpeper to Colonel Nicholas Spencer and Lieutenant Colonel John Washington (the emigrant), great-grandfather of George Washington. From John, the emigrant, his share of the land was bequeathed to his son Lawrence; to his daughter Mildred; from Mildred and her husband, Roger Gregory to her brother Augustine; from Augustine to his son Lawrence (who named the property "Mount Vernon" after Admiral Edward Vernon, of the British navy, under whom Lawrence served in the Cartagena expedition); from Lawrence to his daughter Sarah, with his wife, Ann Fairfax, retaining a life interest in the property; but Sarah dying in childhood, shortly after her father, Mount Vernon reverted to George, the half-brother of Lawrence and the eldest son of Augustine by his second wife. George Washington obtained a legal opinion from James Mercer in 1754 as to his title to Mount Vernon and came into nominal possession that same year by virtue of a rental agreement with Colonel George Lee, who had married Ann Fairfax Washington, the widow of Lawrence. George Washington commenced living at Mount Vernon about March, 1755, and continued to pay a yearly rental for "the use of Mt Vernon tract & Slaves" in discharge of the widow's life interest, through the year 1761. The area of the estate, which was Washington's prized possession, amounted, at the time of his death, to eight thousand and sixty acres, or over twelve square miles of land. Within this area he laid out five distinct farm units, which were named by him: The Mansion House Farm (around Mount Vernon proper); The River Farm (to the northeast of the Mansion and bounded on three sides by Little Hunting Creek and the Potomac River); The Union Farm (southwest of the Mansion and facing Dogue Creek); The Muddy Hole Farm (north of the Mansion, on which Dogue Run takes, or did take, its rise. Its eastern boundary was the narrowed water of Little Hunting Creek); The Dogue Run Farm (which lay along the main branch of Dogue Run to the northwest of the Mansion). A large part of the area in which the farms were laid off was in forest land and a straight line from the Mansion House either in a northeast or northwest direction, to the farthest limits of Washington's property, would have extended four or five miles.

[30]

[3] This lot was bequeathed by Mrs. Washington to her nephew Bartholomew Dandridge.

[4] Mrs. Custis's negroes, who, while they became a part of the Mount Vernon organization, were restricted as to ownership by the terms of the will of Daniel Parke Custis.

[5] All the provisions of the Will respecting the slaves were carried out in full, excepting the educational direction. This failed by reason of the Virginia "black laws" then in force which prohibited schools for the education of negroes. The last of the pensioned slaves died in 1833.

[6] William ("Billy") Lee, was with Washington at the headquarters of the Continental Army throughout the Revolutionary War. In 1785 while assisting Washington in making a survey, he fell and broke one of his knee-pans; three years later, while going for the mail, he fell and broke the other.

[7] The Alexandria Academy building, the corner-stone of which was laid in 1785 by Washington, acting with the Alexandria Lodge of Masons, of which he was a member, is still standing at the corner of Washington and Wolfe streets. In 1786, the trustees of the Academy were incorporated and this bequest fulfilled the arrangement which Washington had made with them in December, 1785. In 1802, after Mrs. Washington's death, the stock so bequeathed was delivered to the trustees; the Bank of Alexandria closed up its affairs in 1833 and, in the course of time, the Academy was succeeded by the Washington School and finally merged with the town's public school system.

[8] This word was undoubtedly meant to be "certainty"; another slip in copying will be noted on page 6, where the superfluous article "a" appears in the 5th line, and on page 22, in the spelling of the word "their."

[9] This letter, dated December 17, 1785, was to the Trustees of the Alexandria Academy, of whom Doctor William Brown, a long-time friend of Washington, was president. In it the General stated that it had long been his intention to place, at his death, £1000 current money of Virginia, in the hands of the trustees, the interest of which was to be used in instituting a school in Alexandria for the education of orphan children who had no resources, or the children of such indigent parents as were unable to give them an education. It not being in the General's power in 1785, to advance the £1000, he would, he said, until he died, or until such time as he could advance the principal, pay the interest thereof, to wit, £50 per annum, in order that "a measure that may be productive of good many not be delayed". The £50 was paid annually from the year 1785 until Washington died; Mrs. Washington continued the payments. After her death, the principal of the fund was delivered to the trustees in 1802 by Washington's executors.

[31]

[10] By act of the Virginia legislature in 1785, the state subscribed 20,000 dollars to the capital stock of the Potomac Company and a like amount to the James River Navigation Company, which amounts purchased 50 shares in the former company and 100 shares in the latter, in the name of George Washington as a testimony to his unexampled merits. Embarrassed by this action, Washington wrote to Governor Patrick Henry, expressing his appreciation, but begged that the act might have no effect so far as his private emolument was concerned, but if the legislature should be pleased to allow him to convert the shares so granted to objects of a public nature it would be his study to prove his gratitude by the best selection of such objects. The legislature forthwith passed an act appropriating the shares and profits therefrom to such objects of a public nature as Washington should direct during his lifetime, or designate by his last Will and Testament.

[11] The national university project never materialized. It had been proposed in the Constitutional Convention of 1787, as one of the expressed powers of Congress, but failed of being incorporated in that document. While President of the United Sates, Washington recommended it to Congress in his address to that body, January 8, 1790, and through his efforts a site was reserved in the new capital city for such an university. Nothing further was done, though the project was sponsored by Presidents Jefferson and Madison. The Potomac Navigation Company failed in 1828 and the shares became valueless.

[12] The name originally was the Augusta Academy, so-called from the Virginia county in which it was located. It was renamed Liberty Hall in the charter obtained in 1782, when the institution was relocated near Lexington, in the Shenandoah Valley. In 1795 the Virginia legislature approved Washington's intention of assigning the Potomac Company shares to a national university and requested him to assign, in like manner, the James River Company shares to the Liberty Hall Academy. This he did in a letter to the Governor of Virginia in September, 1796. In 1798 the name Liberty Hall was changed to Washington College and, after a fire in 1803, the institution moved into the town of Lexington. After General Robert E. Lee's presidency (1865-1870), the name was changed to Washington and Lee University. Although the James River Navigation Company long ago passed out of existence, this fund was salvaged in time, is still existent and forms a part of the University endowment which is cherished far beyond its present financial worth.

[13] The education of these two boys proved something of a worry to Washington and their thoughtless and irresponsible conduct drew from him to them several, almost sharp, letters.

[32]

[14] Betty Lewis Carter, daughter of the General's only sister, Betty and Fielding Lewis, of Fredericksburg.

[15] William Augustine Washington, son of the General's half-brother Augustine (who was called by the General "Austin").

[16] The words "and his heirs" were interpolated by Washington through inadvertence in reading over this page, as he had already incorporated the necessary legal provision after the parenthesis; then, rather than make an erasure or recopy the page, he let them stand.

[17] This lottery was held by Colonel William Byrd, in Williamsburg in the year 1768. Washington won seven prizes, amounting in all to 568½ acres. The town of Edenburgh, in Prince George County, no longer exists.

[18] Bushrod Washington, the eldest son of John Augustine (the General's favorite brother, who had died in 1787), and the most "bookish" of the General's nephews. The surviving papers, which suffered inexcusable spoilation while in Bushrod's possession, were sold to the United States in 1834 and 1849 by George Corbin Washington, Bushrod's nephew, son of Jane and William Augustine. They are now in the custody of the Library of Congress. Some 455 books and 750 pamphlets were sold in 1847 or 48 to Henry Stevens and purchased from him by some Boston gentlemen to prevent their being taken to England. They are now in the custody of the Boston Athenaeum, which has published a catalogue of them.

[19] The terms of the contracts for the purchase of these lands were not fulfilled during Mrs. Washington's lifetime. The Pennsylvania land was sold in 1808 to Andrew Parks, who had married Harriott Washington, a daughter of Samuel. The New York Mohawk land was sold in 1803 to George Steptoe Washington. The Dismal Swamp property had been sold in 1795 to General Henry Lee. It was reconveyed back to the estate in 1809 through the inability of Lee to meet the terms of the sale. In 1825 it was purchased by Bushrod Washington, by him devised to his wife, and on her death to his nephews and grand-nephews.

[20] The Gloucester County land was sold to Burwell Bassett for the benefit of the children of George Augustine Washington, son of the General's brother Charles.

[21] The Great Kanawha lands were divided by agreement, among the legatees of the Washington estate in 1805, by a deed of partition, executed and filed in the Fairfax County court.

[22] The Difficult Run land was purchased by William Sheppard some little time before Washington's death. The last payment was made thereon to the executors of the estate in 1811.

[33]

[23] David Steuart Erskine, eleventh Earl of Buchan. He originated the Society of Antiquarians of Scotland. The box had been brought to America in 1791 by Archibald Robertson, a mediocre Scotch painter, who was commissioned to paint a portrait of Washington for the Earl. Robertson painted a miniature, from life, in New York in 1791 and from the miniature a portrait in oils, which was finished and sent to the Earl in 1792. In 1804 Buchan returned the box to President Jefferson, for the National University, which was never established. The present location of the box cannot be established with certainty.

[24] Benjamin Franklin's Will provided that "My fine crabtree walking stick, with a gold head, curiously wrought in the form of a cap of liberty, I give to my friend, and the friend of mankind, General Washington. If it were a sceptre he has merited it; and would become it. It was a present to me from that excellent woman Madame de Forbach, the Dowager Duchess of DeuxPonts, connected with some verses which should go with it." The cane was presented to the United States in 1843 by Samuel Thornton Washington, grandson of Charles, and is now in the Washington Collection in the National Museum of American History.

[25] Lawrence and Robert Washington were descendants of Lawrence, the brother of John, the emigrant. He settled in the Chotank region, which was a rather vaguely defined area on the south bank of the Potomac, some miles north of Westmoreland. Lawrence and Robert belonged to the Lund and Townsend branch of the Washingtons and were the playmates of George, after his father's death, when he, seemingly, was not settled in any one particular place, but spent much of his time away from the "Ferry Farm" near Fredericksburg, in long visits with different relatives, before finally settling permanently with his half-brother Lawrence, at Mount Vernon. The cane and spyglass bequeathed to Lawrence have been returned to Mount Vernon. The cane bequeathed to Robert is at the Morristown National Historical Park, a bequest from Lloyd W. Smith.

[26] Doctor James Craik, two years Washington's senior, served with him in the Fort Necessity campaign, 1754, in the capacity of surgeon and was also with the Virginia troops in the ill-starred Braddock expedition. He was Chief Physician and Surgeon in the Continental Army during the Revolutionary War. He was one of the three physicians attendant on Washington in his last illness. The tambour secretary and circular chair have been restored to Mount Vernon and are now in their accustomed places in General Washington's Study.

[27] Doctor David Stuart, of Fairfax County, a warm friend of Washington, was appointed by him a member of the first Board of Commissioners for the District of Columbia. He married Eleanor Calvert Custis, the widow of John Parke Custis, Washington's step-son. The telescope and dressing table are back at Mount Vernon in the General's Study where they stood originally.

[34]

[28] Bryan Fairfax was four years the junior of Washington, but an unbroken friendship always existed between them. Although not wholly in sympathy with the Revolution, he was not a firm loyalist. He refused to take the oath of allegiance to the King in 1777. He helped organize the Episcopal Church in Virginia after the Revolution, joined the ministry in 1789, and officiated at Christ Church, Alexandria and the Falls Church in Fairfax County. He lived at "Mount Eagle", near Alexandria and died there in 1802. He became Lord Fairfax (eighth) in 1793. The Bible is now preserved in the Library of Congress. Washington was mistaken about the Bible having been given him by the Bishop of Sodor and Man; it had been bequeathed to him by the son of the Bishop, whose name being the same as that of his father, accounts for the error.

[29] Marie Jean Paul Roche Yves Gilbert du Motier, Marquis de Lafayette, (Washington always wrote it Fayette) was twenty-five years Washington's junior yet, despite the difference of age, the friendship between the two men became strong and lasting. The young nobleman's enthusiasm, idealism and faith in the cause of liberty, aside from his engaging personality, appealed strongly to the older man who came to love Lafayette as a son. This bequest shows Washington's complete understanding of the romantic sentiment that formed so large a part of Lafayette's character. A pair of steel pistols preserved at Chateaux Lafayette at Charaniac-Lafayette, Haute-Loire, France, are believed to be those bequeathed by Washington to Lafayette.

[30] Hannah (Bushrod), the widow of John Augustine Washington; Mildred (Thornton), the widow of Charles; Eleanor (Calvert) Custis Stuart, the widow of John Parke Custis; Hannah (Fairfax), of "Fairfield", widow of Warner Washington; and Elizabeth (Foote) Washington, of "Hayfield", the widow of Lund Washington, the manager of Mount Vernon during the Revolutionary War. Mourning rings were a social custom in the 18th century and such bequests were not unusual. One of these Washington mourning rings is known to have survived.

[31] Tobias Lear, of New Hampshire, came to Mount Vernon well recommended; after the Revolution be became the trusted friend of Washington. His second wife was Fanny Bassett, niece of Martha Washington and the young widow of George Augustine Washington; after her death Lear married Frances Dandridge Henley, also the niece of Mrs. Washington. He was Secretary to the President of the United States in Washington's first administration and military secretary at Mount Vernon during the French War excitement in 1798-1799.

[32] Sally Ball Haynie, a grand daughter of Mary Ball's older half-sister Elizabeth Johnson Bonom Straughan and pensioner of Mary Ball, the mother of Washington. The General continued to aid her financially, after his mother's death. This legacy was paid to her in 1801.

[33] Thomas Bishop and John Alton were servants from Colonial times. Bishop had been a servant of General Braddock and came to Washington after that General's death in 1755. Alton had accompanied Washington on his trip from Virginia to Boston in 1756 and prepared Mount Vernon for the homecoming of the Colonel and Mrs. Washington, after their marriage.

[34] William Augustine Washington (son of the General's half-brother Augustine—"Austin"). The sword which fell to him is now in the New York State Library, Albany. When the State Capitol was burned in 1911, this sword was badly damaged. It was a rapier with a filigree handle and guard and white sharkskin scabbard. It is said to have been the handsomest sword owned by the General.

George Lewis (son of the General's only sister). The sword chosen by him is now at Mount Vernon. It is said to be the sword Washington wore when he resigned his commission at Annapolis in 1783, when he was inaugurated President of the United States in 1789, and on other state and dress occasions.

George Steptoe Washington (son of the General's brother Samuel). The sword chosen by him is now at Mount Vernon. This sword was presented to Washington in 1796 by Theophilus Alte, of Solingen, Prussia. It is a handsome weapon, wide of blade and rather heavy looking, with an ornate scabbard.

Bushrod Washington (son of the General's brother John Augustine). The sword chosen by him is now at Mount Vernon. It is a Spanish dress sword with a gilt hilt and hilt mounted black leather scabbard and is described as a "mourning sword".

Samuel Washington (son of the General's brother Charles). The sword chosen by him is now in the National Museum of American History, Washington, D. C. It is the sword worn by the General during the Revolution and is a "cutteau" with a slightly curved blade and a green colored, deeply grooved ivory hilt, wound with silver strips; the short quillons are silver mounted. The scabbard is of russet leather, silver mounted and marked "J. Bailey Fishkill". Bailey describes himself as a black and whitesmith and cutler of New York City, which place he left when the British captured it in 1776. He moved to Fredricksburg, N. Y., and, later, to Fishkill. His mark fixes the approximate date of the scabbard as coming into Washington's possession about 1779 or 1780. The date of the sword is as yet undetermined. It is, however, known as the "service sword" from its having been used by Washington during the Revolutionary War.

[35] John Augustine Washington, the General's best loved brother, looked after Washington's interests at Mount Vernon, during the French and Indian War.

[36] The area of the present Mount Vernon (less than 500 acres) formed a part of this bequest to Bushrod Washington. A nice legal question of title to the Mount

Vernon property, bequeathed contingently by Lawrence Washington to his half-brother George, came into view at the time of the General's death, as by Lawrence's will, if George died childless the property was to revert to Augustine ("Austin") or his heirs. There was no doubt of the title at the time George took possession; nevertheless, because of the law of entail, then in force in Virginia, Washington obtained authoritative, legal opinions as to his title in 1754, two years after the death of Lawrence, and again in 1769, but failed to follow the suggestion in this latter opinion (by Edmund Pendleton) that the entail in the estate be "docked" by legislative action, in the doing of which Pendleton "could see no impropriety". When Washington made this Will in 1799, Virginia had long since abolished all entails and he apparently took it for granted that any question of an "entail" in Mount Vernon had been automatically settled. At any rate the bequests to the heirs of his half-brother Augustine ("Austin") of four twenty-thirds of the cash value of that portion of the entire estate so converted, amply compensated them for any presumptive claims they may have had to the Mount Vernon real estate. Their failure to protest at the time of the final settlement by the executors made any question that might be raised thereafter a purely academic one.

[37] Thomson Mason, a son of George Mason, of "Gunston Hall".

[38] Humphrey Peake died in 1785.

[39] George Augustine Washington (son of Charles) died in 1793. He was a cornet, ensign, lieutenant, and captain in the 3d Continental Dragoons. He acted for a time during the Revolutionary War as a volunteer aide to his uncle; he afterwards became an aide to the Marquis de Lafayette. He married Fanny Bassett and, in Washington's first term as President, managed Mount Vernon and its farms. He seems to have been the only one of the General's nephews who had a liking for agriculture. His sons were George Fayette and Charles (not Lawrence) Augustine Washington. This slip in identity may have been due to the impress made on Washington's mind by the conduct of George Steptoe and Lawrence Augustine, as well as the strain of copying so long a document as the Will.

[40] Eleanor Parke ("Nelly") Custis, who marred Lawrence Lewis, at Mount Vernon, February 22, 1799, and George Washington Parke Custis, two of the children of John Parke Custis. There has been some confusion respecting the adoption of them by Washington. They were looked upon by the General as his wards and George Washington Parke Custis is so mentioned, later, in the Will, but the General seems never to have bothered to legally confirm this status, except in the case of Nelly Custis. On January 23, 1799, the General wrote to Lawrence Lewis: "Your letter of the 10th instant I received in Alexandria, on

Monday, whither I went to become the guardian of Nelly, thereby to authorize a license for your nuptials on the 22d of next month."

[41] The house erected by Lawrence Lewis shortly after 1800 on this land, from plans of Dr. William Thornton, the architect of the United States Capitol building, was named "Woodlawn". It has been restored and is still standing. A portion of the land, like that of the Mount Vernon area bequeathed to Bushrod Washington (with the exception of the present Mount Vernon property), has been subdivided into many small holdings.

[42] The grist mill was located at the head of Dogue Creek and is shown on the map of Mount Vernon made by Washington in 1793, reproductions of which are available in numerous publications. The Distillery was near the Mill. As early as 1761 Washington purchased a 50 gallon still from England, but distilling on a large scale was not undertaken until about 1796 or 1797.

[43] The "Four Mile Run Tract" was on the north bank of that stream and extended toward the "Arlington" estate, which Custis had inherited from his father. After the Civil War, Major General George Washington Custis Lee conveyed over 300 acres of the "Four Mile Run" land to the Episcopal Theological Seminary at Arlington. The remainder of the property has been subdivided into farms and building lots under numerous ownerships.

[44] Square 21 in Washington City is bounded by 25th, 26th, D and E Streets, Northwest. Custis neglected to take the steps necessary to confirm his title, though he bequeathed the square to Colonel Robert E. Lee, who had married his daughter Mary Ann Randolph Custis. In 1830 this property was sold for the nonpayment of taxes through an authority created by Congress, a short while before 1830.

[45] This portion of the estate which was the residue to be divided into twenty-three equal parts after Mrs. Washington's death, was valued in the "Schedule" at $530,000. The estate already devised has been calculated at $250,000, which figure excluded any estimate of the value of the 124 slaves at Mount Vernon, but as these were to be given their freedom later they could not properly be considered in any estimate.

[46] Augustine ("Austin") Washington, the General's half-brother, died in 1762. His daughter Elizabeth had married General Alexander Spotswood. Jane had married Colonel John Thornton. Ann had married Burdett Ashton. Augustine's son, William Augustine Washington, was generally referred to as "of Wakefield".

[47] Washington spelled her name oftener Harriet and she signed herself Harriott. She had married Andrew Parks.

[38]

[48] Jane Washington had married William Augustine Washington, "of Wakefield".

[49] Frances Washington had married Burgess Ball. Mildred had married Thomas Hammond.

[50] Maria, then unmarried, was Anna Maria Washington.

[51] Elizabeth ("Eliza") Parke Custis had married Thomas Law. Martha Parke Custis had married Thomas Peter. Eleanor ("Nelly") Parke Custis had married Lawrence Lewis.

[52] The ward, grandson of Mrs. Washington, was George Washington Parke Custis.

[53] This advice would have been sound but for the unforseen invention of the steam locomotive, which completely changed the whole system of land transportation.

[54] This new vault was built by Lawrence Lewis and George Washington Parke Custis in 1830-1. The old vault had been built by the General in fulfillment of the wish expressed in the will of Lawrence, his half-brother, and it was in the old vault the General's remains reposed from 1799 to 1831. The location was "improper" mainly because of numerous springs in the slope which caused landslides, some of them of a serious nature. This danger also threatened the Mansion House, though it is doubtful if the General had become aware of it. It has been checked by a tunnel and modern drainage system.

[55] Washington died on a Saturday night and the funeral was arranged for the following Wednesday. Before that day so many friends, near neighbors and acquaintances, both in Virginia and Maryland announced their intention of being present that all thought of a private funeral was abandoned. A lead-lined mahogany casket, with an enclosing box, lined and covered with black cloth, was made in Alexandria and on Wednesday morning, December 18, Washington's body was brought from the large room at the north end of the house to the veranda, on the river front of the Mansion House and there lay in state until about three o'clock in the afternoon. By then all arrangements had been completed and the procession, led by the military from Alexandria, moved to the tomb, around the north end of the house past the front door. The soldiery consisted of militia horse, artillery and infantry, commanded by Colonel George Deneale. The band, which followed the infantry, played a dirge; a group of clergy consisting of the Reverend Thomas Davis, of Christ Church, Alexandria, Reverend James Muir and Reverend William Maffitt, of the Presbyterian Church, and Reverend William Dulany Addison of the Episcopalian Church at Oxon Hill, Maryland, immediately preceded the bier, which was borne by lieutenants

[39]

of the militia, with Colonels Charles Little, Charles Simms, William Payne, George Gilpin, Dennis Ramsay and Philip Marsteller as honorary pall-bearers. Colonel Thomas Blackburn walked at the head of the bier, behind which Washington's horse, fully caparisoned, was led by two of the servants. Relatives followed (none of the accounts mention Mrs. Washington); eight officers and forty-eight members of Masonic Lodge 22, of Alexandria, fifteen members of Lodge 47, of Alexandria and a committee of three or four from Lodge 15 of Washington, D. C. The Mayor and Commonality of Alexandria followed and a concourse of citizens which the Alexandria *Gazette* stated was "immense". At the vault the troops formed a lane through which the procession passed. The Reverend Mr. Davis read the burial service and delivered a brief address; the Masonic rites were performed by Doctor Elisha Cullen Dick, minute guns were fired from Mr. Robert Hamilton's schooner, which came down from Alexandria and anchored off Mount Vernon, and the ceremonies concluded with the firing of salutes by the artillery, infantry and horse. Washington's body remained in the old vault until 1831, when the present tomb was finished and all the bodies then in the old vault were removed to the present location. The marble sarcophagi, in which rest the remains of the General and Mrs. Washington, were carved and presented by John Struthers, of Philadelphia.

[56] The word "through" is an inadvertence which shows how physically tired Washington had become in the last year of his life; the examples of his properly spelling the word "throw" in his writings are too many to admit of any other explanation.

[57] There were no disputes over the provisions of the Will. A minor controversy was carried into court, but this was unconnected with the direct bequests.

[58] The inadvertence in omitting the word "nine" from the date of the year is another indication of the physical weariness mentioned above.

Schedule of property comprehended in the foregoing Will, which is directed to be sold, and some of it, conditionally is sold; with discriptive, and explanatory notes[1] relative thereto.

In Virginia

	acres	price	dollars

Loudon County

Difficult run	300	.... 6,666 (a)

(a) This tract for the size of it is valuable,—more for its situation than the quality of its soil, though that is good for Farming; with a considerable portion of grd—that might, very easily, be improved into Meadow.—It lyes on the great road from the City of Washington, Alexandria and George Town, to Leesburgh & Winchester; at Difficult bridge,—nineteen miles from Alexandria,—less from the City & George Town, and not more than three from Matildaville at the Great Falls of Potomac.—There is a valuable seat on the Premises—and the whole is conditionally sold—for the sum annexed in the Schedule [*See the notes to the Will in reference to this property.*]

Loudoun & Fauquier

Ashbys Bent	2481	...... $10	 24,810	(b)
Chattins Run	885	 8	 7,080	

(b) What the selling prices of lands in the vicinity of these two tracts are, I know not; but compared with those above the ridge, and others below them, the value annexed will appear moderate— a less one would not obtain them from me.[2]

[41]

Berkeley

So fork of Bullskin .. 1600
Head of Evans's M .. 453
On Wormeley's line .. 183

2236 . . . . . . 20 . . . . . 44.720 (c)

(c) The surrounding land, not superior in Soil, situation or properties of any sort, sell currently at from twenty to thirty dollars an Acre.—The lowest price is affixed to these[3]

Frederick

Bought from Mercer . 571 . . . . . . 20 . . . . . 77.420 (d)

(d) The observations made in the last note applies equally to this tract tract; being in the vicinity of them, and of similar quality, altho' it lyes in another County[4]

Hampshire

On Potk River
above B . . . . 240 . . . . . . 15 . . . . . 3.600 (e)

(e) This tract, though small, is extremely valuable.—It lyes on Potomac River about 12 miles above the Town of Bath (or Warm springs) and is in the shape of a horse Shoe;—the river running almost around it.—Two hundred Acres of it is rich low grounds; with a great abundance of the largest & finest Walnut trees; which, with the produce of the Soil, might (by means of the improved Navigation of the Potomac) be brought to a shipping port with more ease, and at a smaller expence, than that which is transported 30 miles only by land.

Gloucester

On North River . . . . . 400 . . . . abt . . . . 3.600 (f)

(f) This tract is of second rate Gloucester low grounds.—It has no Improvements thereon, but lyes on navigable water, abounding in

[42]

Fish and Oysters. It was received in payment of a debt (carrying interest) and valued in the year 1789 by an impartial Gentleman to £800.—NB. It has lately been sold, and there is due thereon, a balance equal to what is annexed the Schedule[6]

Nansemond

Near Suffolk ⅓ of 1119 acres.... } .. 373...... 8 .... 2.984 (g)

(g) These 373 acres are the third part of undivided purchases made by the deceased Fielding Lewis Thomas Walker and myself; on full conviction that they would become valuable.—The land lyes on the Road from Suffolk to Norfolk—touches (if I am not mistaken) some part of the Navigable water of Nansemond River—borders on, and comprehends part of the rich Dismal Swamp;—is capable of great improvement;—and from its situation must become extremely valuable.[7]

Great Dismal Swamp

My dividend thereof .... abt .... 20.000 (h)

(h) This is an undivided Interest wch—I held in the Great Dismal Swamp Company—containing about 4000 acres, with my part of the Plantation & Stock thereon belonging to the Company in the sd Swamp[8]

Ohio River

Round bottom	587
Little Kanhawa	2314
16 miles lowr down	2448
Opposite Big Bent	4395

9744 .. 10 .... 97 440 (i)

(i) These several tracts of land are of the first quality on the Ohio River, in the parts where they are situated;—being almost if not altogether River bottoms.—The smallest of these tracts is actually sold at ten dollars an acre but the consideration therefor not received—the rest are equally valuable & will sell as high—especially that which lyes just below the little Kanhawa and is opposite to a thick settlement on the West side of the Rivr.—The four tracts have an aggregate breadth upon the River of Sixteen miles and is bounded thereby that distance.[9]

Great Kanhawa

Near the Mouth West	10990
East side above	7276
Mouth of Cole River	2000
Opposite thereto	2950
Burning Spring	125

23341 .... 200.000 (k)

(k) These tracts are situated on the Great Kanhawa River, and the first four are bounded thereby for more than forty miles.—It is acknowledged by all who have seen them (and of the tract containing 10990 acres which I have been on myself, I can assert) that there is no richer, or more valuable land in all that Region;—They are conditionally sold for the sum mentioned in the Schedule—that is $200.000 and if the terms of that Sale are not complied with they will command considerabley more.—The tract of which the 125 acres is a moiety, was taken up by General Andrew Lewis and myself for, and on account of a bituminous Spring which it contains, of so inflamable a nature as to burn as freely as spirits, and is as nearly difficult to extinguish.[10]

Maryland

Charles County	600	....	6	..... 3.600	(i)
Montgomery Do	519	....	12	..... 6.228	(m)

(I) I am but little acquainted with this land, although I have once been on it.—It was received (many years since) in discharge of a debt due to me from Daniel Jenifer Adams at the value annexed

[44]

thereto—and must be worth more.—It is very level, lyes near the River Potomac.[11]

(m) This tract lyes about 30 miles above the City of Washington, not far from Kittoctan.—It is good farming Land, and by those who are well acquainted with it I am informed that it would sell at twelve or $15 per. acre.[12]

Pennsylvania

Great Meadows ..... 234....... 6 ..... 1.404 (n)

(n) This land is valuable on account of its local situation, and other properties.—It affords an exceeding good stand on Braddocks road from Fort Cumberland to Pittsburgh—and besides a fertile soil, possesses a large quantity of natural Meadow, fit for the scythe.—It is distinguished by the appellation of the Great Meadows—where the first action with the French in the year 1754 was fought.[13]

New York

Mohawk River abt. .. 1000..... 6 .....6.00 (o)

(o) This is the moiety of about 2000 Acs. which remains unsold of 6071 Acres on the Mohawk River (Montgomery Cty) in a Patent grated to Daniel Coxe in the Township of Coxeborough & Carolana—as will appear by Deed from Marinus Willet & wife to George Clinton (late Governor of New York) and myself.—The latter sales have been at Six dollars an acr; and what remains unsold will fetch that or more[14]

North Westn. Territy

On little Miami 839
Ditto 977
Ditto 1235

———

3051 ...... 5 ..... 15.251 (p)

(p) The quality of these lands & their Situation, may be known by

[45]

the Surveyors Certificates—which are filed along with the Patents.—They lye in the vicinity of Cincinnati;—one tract near the mouth of the little Miami—another seven & the third ten miles up the same—I have been informed that they will readily command more than they are estimated at.[15]

Kentucky

Rough Creek 3000
Ditto adjoining 2000

——————

5000 ...... 2 ..... 10.000 (q)

(q) For the description of these tracts in detail, see General Spotswoods letters, filed with the other papers relating to them.—Besides the General good quality of the Land, there is a valuable Bank of Iron Ore thereon:—which, when the settlement becomes more populus (and settlers are moving that way very fast) will be found very valuable; as the rough Creek, a branch of Green River affords ample water for Furnaces & forges.[16]

Lots—viz.

City of Washington

Two, near the Capital, Sqr 634 cost $963 } 15 000 (r)
—and with Buildgs

No. 5. 12. 13. & 14—the 3 last, Water lots on the Eastern Branch, in Sqr. } . 4.132 (s)
667. containing together 34.438 sqr. feet a 12 Cts.

(r) The two lots near the Capital, in square 634, cost me 963$ only; but in this price I was favoured, on condition that I should build two Brick houses three Story high each:—without this reduction the selling prices of those Lots would have cost me about $1350.—These lots, with the buildings thereon, when completed will stand me in $15000 at least.[18]

[46]

(s) Lots No. 5. 12. 13 & 14 on the Eastn. branch, are advantageously situated on the water—and although many lots much less convenient have sold a great deal higher I will rate these at 12 Cts—the square foot only.[19]

Alexandria

Corner of Pitt & Prince Sts—half an Acre— laid out into buildgs—3 or 4 of wch. are let on grd. Rent at $3 pr. foot   } . 4.000 (t)

(t) For this lot, though unimproved, I have refused $3500.—It has since been laid off into proper sized lots for building on—three or 4 of which are let on ground Rent—forever—at three dollars a foot on the Street.—and this price is asked for both fronts on Pitt & Princes Street.[20]

Winchester

A lot in the Town of half an Acr & another in the Commons of about 6 Acs— supposed   } . .400 (u)

(u) As neither the lot in the Town or Common have any improvements on them, it is not easy to fix a price, but as both are well situated, it is presumed the price annexed to them in the Schedule is a reasonable valun.[21]

Bath—or Warm Springs

Two Well situated, & had buildings to the amt of £150   } . . 800 (w)

(w) The Lots in Bath (two adjoining) cost me, to the best of my recollection, betwn. fifty & sixty pounds 20 years ago;—and the buildings thereon £150 more.—Whether property there has increased or decreased in its value, and in what condition the houses are, I am ignorant. but suppose they are valued too high[22]

Stock[23]

United States .....6 pr Cts 3746
Do defered...... 1873
3 pr Cts......... 2946 } 2500   6.246 (x)

(x) These are the sums which are actually funded.—And though no more in the aggregate than $7.566—stand me in at least ten thousand pounds in Virginia money.—being the amount of bonded and other debts due to me, & discharged during the War when money had depreciated in that ratio—and was so settled by public authoty—

Potomack Company

24 Shares—cost ea £100 Sterg .... 20.666 (y)

(y) The value annexed to these sha: is what they have actually cost me, and is the price affixed by Law:—and although the present selling price is under par, my advice to the Legatees (for whose benefit they are intended, especially those who can afford to lye out of the money) is that each should take and hold one;—there being a moral certainty of a great and increasing profit arising from them in the course of a few years—

James River Company

5 Shares—each cost $100 .... 500 (z)

(z) It is supposed that the Shares in the James River Company must also be productive.—But of this I can give no decided opinion for want of more accurate informatn.

Bank of Columbia

170 Shares—$40 each 6.800

Bank of Alexandria

—besides 20 to the Free School 5   1.000 } (&)

(&) These are nominal prices of the Shares of the Banks of Alexandria & Columbia—the selling prices vary according to circumstances. But as the Stock usually divided from eight to ten per cent per annum, they must be worth the former—at least—so long as the Banks are conceived to be Secure, though from circumstances may, sometimes be below it.[24]

Stock—living—viz.—

1 Covering horse, 5 Coh. Horses—4 riding do—Six brood Mares—20 working horses & mares.—2 Covering Jacks—& 3 young ones—10 she Asses, 42 working Mules—15 younger ones 329 head of horned Cattle 640 head of Sheep—and a large Stock of Hogs—the pricise number unknown	15.653
☞ My Manager has estimated this live stock at £7,000 but I shall set it down in order to make rd sum at	

Aggregate amt. $530.000

The value of the live stock depends more upon the quality than quantity of the different species of it, and this again upon the demand, and judgment or fancy of purchasers.[25]

G. Washington

Mount Vernon
9th. July 1799

GW
NOTES TO THE SCHEDULE OF PROPERTY

[1] The "Schedule of property" accompanies the Will and, like it, is entirely in Washington's writing. The "Notes", also in Washington's writing, explanatory of the items and their values were lettered by him, parenthetically, as given, but placed by Washington in a group at the end of the "Schedule". In this publication they are placed directly after each item for clarity and the greater convenience of the reader.

[2] The Ashby's Bent and Chattin Run tracts were obtained in part, by purchase from Bryan Fairfax. They were on the east slope of the Blue Ridge, near Upperville. Washington's estimate both of the quantity and value of the land was inexact. The Ashby's Bent tract actually contained 2690 acres and was sold for $8820. to General Spotswood; the Chattin Run land amounted to 1240 acres and was sold to Colonel Thornton for $9920. The over estimate was thus $13,157.

[3] The Berkeley lands were in the southern part of what is now Jefferson County, West Virginia. The Bullskin tracts were found to amount to 2478 acres in all and were sold to Andrew Parks, Corbin Washington's heirs, Burdett Ashton and Robert Lewis for $36,733. This was $4425. below Washington's valuation even though the quantity was 301 acres more than he estimated.

[4] The Frederick tract, obtained from either James or Col. George Mercer, was actually short by 17 acres and was bought by Lawrence Lewis for $8969. which was $3452. less than the estimate. This tract became "Audley", (near Berryville, now Clarke County, Virginia) the home of Nelly Custis Lewis, who lived there until her death. Repetition of the word tract was a pen slip.

[5] The Hampshire land extended over 246 acres and was sold to Samuel Washington for $4999., exceeded the estimate by $1399.

[50]

[6] The Gloucester tract had been sold to George Ball and the balance of $3600. was due on the purchase. This balance was not paid and, in 1805, the land was re-sold to the children of George Augustine Washington for $3836.

[7] The Nansemond lands were one-third of a joint holding by Washington, Colonel Fielding Lewis and Doctor Thomas Walker. The Washington interest was sold by George Washington Parke Custis, acting as an executor, to William B. Whitehead, in 1851, for $290. or about 75¢ an acre. Washington estimated this land at about $8. an acre.

[8] Washington owned two of the twenty-one shares of the Great Dismal Swamp Company. He valued them at £5000 in 1793. The Dismal Swamp property was sold to General Henry Lee ("Light Horse Harry" of the Revolution and the father of Robert E. Lee). He was unable to meet the payments agreed upon and, in 1799, relinquished the purchase. After its reconveyance back to the Washington estate in 1809, dividends varying from $580. to $2400. were paid annually by the company for about fifteen years. *(See notes to the Will.)*

[9-10] The Ohio River land, known as Round Bottom, was Washington's portion of the lands granted by Governor Dinwiddie to the Virginia troops, officers and men, who had served in the French and Indian War. In 1770 Washington and Colonel William Crawford, one of America's famous frontiersmen, located these lands in a canoe trip of some 500 miles. Washington was delegated by a meeting of the officers in 1771 to establish this granted land and push the business of titles thereto. It was a cooperative scheme, so far as the expenses were concerned, but in the end much of the expense had to be met by Washington. Crawford, later, made surveys for the individual claims and Washington, in collaboration with Crawford, platted the same for record. In 1798, Archibald McClean, of Alexandria, offered to purchase the Round Bottom tract and entered into a purchase agreement at $5870., payable in installments. It later developed that this tract actually contained, instead of the 587 acres noted by Washington, 1293 acres. Claims against this tract, on account of its value, by Michael Cresap and a certain Tomlinson, were fought by McClean for years in the courts. In part payment for this land McClean conveyed to the executors of Washington's estate in 1813, a lot in Alexandria, on Wolfe, Water (now Lee), and Potomac streets. No other consideration was ever paid by McClean. To whom the executors sold this property is not known. Washington's remaining lands on the Great and Little Kanawha rivers were divided by the deed of partition entered into by the heirs in 1805, which alloted areas, averaging 1200 acres, to each. How and when these 23 parcels were later disposed of is of little interest to the Washington estate.

[11] The Charles County land in Durham parish, the southwestern section of Charles County, opposite Maryland Point in Virginia. It came to Washington in cancellation of a debt from Daniel Jenifer Adams. Washington's Ledger of Accounts for December 1775, notes this land as being 552⅓ acres. In 1806, Bushrod Washington, as trustee, sold this property to Nicholas Fitzhugh, who "satisfied the balance of the purchase money after deducting the sum due his wife (Sarah, the daughter of Burdett Ashton) as a legatee of George Washington, in part discharge of a debt due from sd. George Washington decd. to David Stewart (Stuart)."

[12] The Montgomery County land was accepted by Washington from the estate of John Francis Mercer, in 1794, in cancellation of a debt, Washington paying the excess of the land value over the debt total of 3633 Spanish milled dollars. This land is about twelve miles north of Rockville, the county seat of Montgomery County, and was known in 1798 as "Woodstock Manor". Through court proceedings this land was sold in 1806 to Thomas Peter for $6446.

[13] The Great Meadows land was purchased by Captain William Crawford for Washington, in 1770, after Washington returned from the trip down the Ohio River, that year. On this tract of 234 acres was the site of Fort Necessity, where Washington surrendered to the French in 1754. It was sold to Andrew Parks and has now become a public park in which a replica of Fort Necessity has been erected.

[14] The Mohawk River land was bought in partnership with Governor George Clinton, in 1783, and was disposed of, in part, before the drawing up of the Will. The remainder, stated by Washington to be 1000 acres was, in reality, 1126 acres and when sold in 1803-6 and 1808, brought the total amount obtained for this land up to $6,600. These sales divided the property into 26 or more parcels.

[15] The Northwest Territory land was acquired by purchase from two Virginia Revolutionary soldiers. Though Washington by Virginia law was entitled to 23,333 acres for his Revolutionary War service, he refused to accept any land on the same principle on which he had declined payment from the Continental Congress, of a salary as Commander-in-Chief of the army. The two tracts purchased were in different townships in Clermont County, Ohio. Owing to changes in the procedure for land entries, occasioned by the states' cessions of the Northwest Territory land to the National Government, it became possible, by sharp practice, to secure title to lands already granted, where the strict letter of a somewhat complicated title procedure had not been meticulously complied with. Washington, his mind occupied with important national concerns, failed to

take the necessary legal steps and his lands were "jumped" by a clever individual, and so lost to the Washington estate.

[16] The Kentucky lands about one hundred miles southwest of Louisville, on the Green River; they are now, after various changes in county lines, in Greyson County. No records have been found showing the transfer of these lands from the Washington estate.

[18] The lots in the city of Washington: Two were near the Capitol square and were purchased, one from the District Commissioners and one from Daniel Carroll of Duddington. They were on the west side of North Capitol Street, slightly to the north of the middle of the block bounded by B and C Streets. Washington paid $964. for the two. The double house which Washington started to erect on the lots was unfinished when he died, but was completed in the year 1800. The houses were burned by the British in 1814 and the lots and the ruins were sold in 1817 to David English for $1446.

[19] The "water lots on the Eastern Branch" of the Potomac (now called the Anacostia River) were purchased by Washington in 1793. They were sold by the executors to Andrew Parks, Thomas Peter and George Steptoe Washington in 1803 for $1,725. which was $2,416. less than Washington's valuation. In 1817, after various court technicalities, created by the differences in law between Virginia and the District of Columbia, had been settled, these water lots were sold to Charles Glover and John G. McDonald for a total of $557.

[20] At a public sale by the executors, in 1803, Doctor T. Peyton bought two of the Alexandria lots for $1172.; Lawrence Augustine Washington bought four lots for $3,831.; Burdett Ashton, one lot for $1206.; and George Steptoe Washington, two lots for $2,426., a total of $8,665. which was double the amount of Washington's valuation.

[21] There seems to be no definite information available as to the fate of these Winchester lots.

[22] The Bath, or Warm Springs property went to Bushrod Washington for $380. where Washington had estimated its value at $800.

[23] The history of these bank and navigation company stocks will be found in the notes to the Will.

[24] The omission here is but another of the indications that the careful copying of the Will and "Schedule" was a tiresome duty. How many drafts of both documents were made before these final ones, it is impossible to say. Indications point to there having been more than two.

[53]

[25] At the executors sales in 1800-2, the total amount obtained for the livestock approximated $12,000. which was $3,600. under Washington's estimate.

THE WILL OF MARTHA WASHINGTON
OF MOUNT VERNON[1]

In the name of God amen

  I Martha Washington of Mount Vernon in the county of Fairfax being of sound mind and capable of disposing of my worldly estate do make ordain and declare this to be my last will and testament hereby revoking all other wills and testaments by me heretofore made.

  Imprimis it is my desire that all my just debts may be punctually paid and that as speedily as the same can be done.

  Item I give and devise to my nephew Bartholomew Dandridge[2] and his heirs my lot in the town of Alexandria situate on Pitt and Cameron streets devised to me by my late husband George Washington deceased.

  Item I give and bequeath to my four nieces Martha W. Dandridge Mary Dandridge Frances Lucy Dandridge and Frances Henley,[3] the debt of two thousand pounds due from Lawrence Lewis and secured by his bond to be equally divided between them or such of them as shall be alive at my death and to be paid to them respectively on the days of their respective marriage or arrival at the age of twenty one years whichsoever shall first happen together with all the interest on said debt remaining unpaid at the time of my death: and in case the whole or

Martha Washington

any part of the said principal sum of two thousand pounds shall be paid to me during my life then it is my will that so much money be raised out of my estate as shall be equal to what I shall have received of the said principal debt and distributed among my four neices aforesaid as herein has been bequeathed, and it is my meaning that the interest accruing after my death on the said sum of two thousand pounds shall belong to my said neices and be equally divided between them or such of them as shall be alive at the time of my death, and be paid annually for their respective uses until they receive their share of the principal.

Item I give and bequeath to my grandson George Washington Parke Custis all the silver plate[4] of every kind of which I shall die possessed, together with the two large plated coolers, the four small plated coolers with the bottle castors, and a pipe of wine if there be one in the house at the time of my death—also the set of Cincinnati tea _{and Table} china,[5] the bowl that has a ship in it, the fine old china jars[6] which usually stand on the chimney piece in the new room: also all the family pictures of every sort[7] and the pictures painted by his sister, and two small skreens worked one by his sister and the other a present from miss Kitty Brown[8]—also his choice of prints[9]—also the two girandoles and lustres[10] that

Martha Washington

stand on them — also the new bedstead which I caused to be made in Philadelphia together with the bed, mattress bolsters & pillows and the white dimity curtains belonging thereto: also two other beds with bolsters and pillows and the white dimity window curtains in the new room — also the iron chest[11] and the desk in the closet which belonged to my first husband; also all my books of every kind except the large bible and prayer book, also the set of tea china that was given to me by Mr. VanBraam every piece having M W on it.[12]

Item   I give and bequeath to my grand daughter Elizabeth Parke Law, the dressing table and glass that stands in the chamber called the yellow room,[13] and Genl. Washington's picture painted by Trumbull.

Item   I give and bequeath to my grand daughter Martha Peter my writing table and the seat to it[14] standing in my chamber, also the print of Genl. Washington that hangs in the passage.

Item   I give and bequeath to my grand daughter Eleanor Parke Lewis the large looking glass in the front Parlour[15] and any other looking glass which she may choose — Also one of the new side board tables in the new room — also twelve chairs with green bottoms to be selected by herself also the marble table in the garrett, also the two prints of the dead soldier,[16] a print

Martha Washington

[57]

of the Washington family in a box in the Garrett and the great chair standing in my chamber,[17] also all the plated ware not hereinafter otherwise bequeathed — also all the sheets table linen, napkins towels, pillow cases remaining in the house at my death, also three beds & bedsteads curtains bolsters and pillows for each bed such as she shall choose and not herein particularly otherwise bequeathed, together with counterpens and a pair of blankets for each bed, also all the wine glasses & decanters[18] of every kind and all the blew and white china in common use.[19]

Item   it is my will and desire that all the wine in bottles in the vaults to be equally divided between my grand daughters and grandson to each of whom I bequeath ten guineas to buy a ring for each.

Item   it is my will and desire that Anna Maria Washington the daughter of my niece to be put in handsome mourning at my death at the expense of my estate and I bequeath to her ten guineas to buy a ring.[20]

Item   I give and bequeath to my neighbor Mrs. Elizabeth Washington[21] five guineas to get something in remembrance of me.

Item   I give and bequeath to Mrs. David Stuart five guineas to buy ^her a ring.[22]

Item   I give and bequeath to Benjamin Lincoln

Martha Washington

[58]

Lear[23] one hundred pounds specie to be vested in funded stock of the United States immediately after my decease and to stand in his name as his property, which investment my executors are to cause to be made.

Item When the vestry of Truro parish shall buy a glebe[24] I devise will and bequeath that my executors shall pay one hundred pounds to them to aid of the purchase, provided the said purchase be made in my lifetime or within three years after my decease.

Item It is my will and desire that all the rest & residue of my estate of whatever kind and description not herein specifically devised or bequeathed shall be sold by the executors of this my last will for ready money as soon after my decease as the same can be done and that the proceeds thereof together with all the money in the house and the debts due me, (the debts due from me and the legacies herein bequeathed being first satisfied) shall be invested by my executors in eight percent stock of the funds of the United States and shall stand on the books in the name of my executors in their character of executors of my will; and it is my desire that the interest there of shall be applied to the proper education of Bartholomew Henley & Samuel Henley the two youngest sons of my sister Henley, and also to the education of John Dandridge son of my deceased nephew John Dandridge so that they may be severally fitted and

Martha Washington

[59]

accomplished in some useful trade and to each of them who shall have lived to finish his education or to reach the age of twenty one years I give and bequeath one hundred pounds to set him up in his trade.

Item my debts and legacies being paid and the education of Bartholomew Henley Samuel Henley and John Dandridge aforesaid being completed, or they being all dead before the completion thereof it is my will and desire that all my estates and interests in whatever form existing whether in money funded stock or any other species of property shall be equally divided among all the persons hereinafter mentioned who shall be living at the time that the interest of the funded stock shall cease to be applicable in pursuance of my will herein before expressed to the education of my nephews Bartholomew Henley Samuel Henley and John Dandridge, namely among Anna Maria Washington, daughter of my niece and John Dandridge son of my nephew and all my great grand children living at the time that the interest of the said funded stock shall cease to be applicable to the education of the said B. Henley S. Henley, and John Dandridge, and the same shall cease to be so applied when all of them shall die before they arrive at the age of twenty one years, or those living shall have finished their education or have arrived at the age of twenty one years, and so long as any one of the three

Martha Washington

lives, who has not finished his education or arrives at the age of twenty one years, the division of the said residuum is to be deferred and no longer.

Lastly I nominate and appoint my grandson, George Washington Parke Custis, my nephews Julius B. Dandridge & Bartholomew Dandridge and my son in law Thomas Peter executors of this my last will and testament. In Witness whereof I have hereunto set my hand and seal this twenty second day of Sept in the year eighteen hundred.

Martha Washington

Sealed signed acknowledged and delivered as her last will and testament in the presence of the subscribing witnesses who have been requested to subscribe the same as such in her presence.

> ROGER FARRELL
> WILLIAM SPENCE
> LAW.ᵉ LEWIS —
> MARTHA PETER,

March 4th 1802

I give to my grandson George Washington Parke Custis my mulatto man Elish — that I bought of mr Butler Washington[25] to him and his hair for ever

Martha Washington

[61]

NOTES FOR
MARTHA WASHINGTON'S WILL

[1] Martha Washington's Will follows so precisely the form of her distinguished husband's that there can be no doubt of that having served as the model. It is in the writing of Eleanor Parke ("Nelly") Custis Lewis, except the title head, which is in a different hand and seems to have been added later. It is signed by Mrs. Washington at the lower right-hand corner of each page and dated by her September 22, 1800, nearly one year after the General died; she added a codicil, in her own handwriting, March 4, 1802. The Will is written on both sides of what are commonly called folio-size sheets (the General's Will is on quarter-size) and covers five pages. Due to the great amount of text per page, the Will is published on seven pages. Martha Washington's revisions, including the insertion of some words, are clearly and accurately denoted.

The Will was probated in the court for Fairfax County, June 21, 1802. It is now, and ever since that date has been, preserved in Fairfax Court House, with the exception of a period of fifty-three years between 1862 and 1915. In the former year the records in Fairfax Court House were seriously damaged through military vandalism, but Martha Washington's Will escaped by a lucky chance and the acquisitive instincts of a lieutenant-colonel of United States troops, who kept possession of it. In 1903 the Will was purchased from the daughter of this officer by Mr. J. Pierpont Morgan, of New York. In 1914 the state of Virginia moved through the Supreme Court of the United States to recover possession of the Will as a muniment of title and importance to the records of the state. Before the case came to an issue however, Mr. Morgan presented the Will to the President of the Supreme Court of Appeals of Virginia and it was at once returned to Fairfax Court House. While in Mr. Morgan's possession the Will was repaired and protected against further disintegration. The pages were inlaid and held together by a binding of ribbon, laced through the left-hand margin of the protecting inlay.

[2] Bartholomew Dandridge (son of the Bartholomew mentioned in the General's Will, who was the brother of Martha) served for a time as Secretary to his uncle, while Washington was President of the United States, and later as his secretary at Mount Vernon. He died in 1802.

[3] Martha Washington Dandridge, Mary Dandridge and Frances Lucy Dandridge, were the daughters of Bartholomew Dandridge, brother of Mrs. Washington. Frances Dandridge Henley was the daughter of Martha's sister Elizabeth Dandridge Aylett Henley.

[4] The Washington plate, nearly every piece of which was marked, either with the Washington arms, or crest, or both, has been much scattered and some lost. As listed intact in the "Inventory &c. of Articles at Mount Vernon" after the General's death (but not returned or recorded in the court of Fairfax County until 1810), it consisted of "44 lb 15 oz Silver plate" and was appraised at $900. Individually the wine coolers, both large and small, were appraised at $60 the pair. The "bottle castors" are listed as "4 Bottle Sliders", presumably so named from their rollers, and valued at only $4., or one dollar each. The wine and other liquors in store at Mount Vernon when the General died are not noted in the "Inventory" as they were all devised to Mrs. Washington. In addition to the Washington plate Custis inherited his father's plate. An impressive amount of Washington/Custis silver is at Mount Vernon, some on loan from Custis's family, as well as other of Martha Washington's descendants.

[5] The words "and Table" have been inserted by Mrs. Washington. The "Cincinnati china" is Chinese export procelain. The principal motif is a winged figure of Fame holding a trumpet in her right hand and in her left, the eagle emblem of the Society of the Cincinnati suspended from a ribbon. The border is blue Fitzhugh. Washington bought the service in 1786 with Colonel Henry ("Light-Horse Harry") Lee acting as agent. Washington's accounts show that on August 23, 1786, he paid $150 for the service numbering 302 pieces. The largest surviving collection of Washington's Cincinnati service is at The Henry Francis du Pont Winterthur Museum. A small collection is on display at Mount Vernon.

[6] The "bowl that has a ship in it" is a large punch bowl whose interior is decorated with a line drawing of a three-masted frigate, *Defender*. The bowl was taken from Arlington House during the Civil War, but is now back at Mount Vernon. It is believed to have been given to Washington by Thomas Truxton, a friend and colleague interested in trade with the orient. The mantel garniture given to George Washington by Samuel Vaughan consisted of three pieces of Worcester porcelain decorated by Jefferyes Hamett O'Neale, have been restored to the "new room" (Washington's large dining room) where they stand on the Italian marble mantel, another gift from Vaughan. Not mentioned among Martha Washington's bequests, but also a gift from Vaughan, is a large painting of the Battle of Minden - apparently intended to hang over the mantel, but in 1799 it had been displaced by a painting entitled "Moonlight" and moved to the Downstairs Bedroom where it now hangs on loan from Washington and Lee University.

[7] The "family pictures of every sort" unquestionably means the portraits. The screens are impossible to identify.

[8] Miss Kitty Brown was the daughter of Doctor William Brown of Alexandria.

[9] The "prints" (engravings) are listed more or less definitely in the "Inventory". Some of them have found their way back to Mount Vernon.

[10] Girandoles were ornate bracket lamps. These "two girandoles" are listed in the "Inventory" as "2 Elegant Lustres" and are appraised at $120.

[11] The iron chest belonging to Daniel Parke Custis (Mrs. Washington's first husband and grandfather of George Washington Parke Custis) is listed in the "Inventory" with its contents of securities (bank stocks, etc.) and other valuables. It was removed from Arlington House to the Patent Office for safe keeping during the Civil War and was returned with other things from Arlington to the Lee family in 1911; in 1954 the Association bought it from the family.

[12] The "china that was given to me by Mr. VanBraam every piece having MW on it" is not listed in the "Inventory". It was presented to Mrs. Washington by Andreas Everardus VanBraam Houckgeest, a Pennsylvania merchant, and one of the earliest American Chinese traders, who had it made and brought it himself from China in 1796. This also is Chinese export porcelain and each piece has an elaborate design in gold and color with the cipher in the center surrounded by a burst of gold rays; the border is a chain of fifteen links with the name of a state within each link. Only a few pieces have survived: two are at Mount Vernon; two are in the White House, Washington, D.C.; three are in the National Museum of American History and one is in the Metropolitan Museum, New York. This china has been extensively but poorly copied.

[13] The Yellow Room now serves as a passageway from the hall at the head of the south stair on the second floor, to the center hall of the Mansion. The dressing table is a four-drawer chest of drawers, the top one fitted with accessory compartments. It has been restored to the Yellow Bedroom. The portrait of General Washington by John Trumbull is at Winterthur.

[14] The print was a proof impression of General Washington presented as a gift to Mrs. Washington in 1797. It is still owned by descendants of Martha Custis Peter. The desk is a French piece bought by Washington for his wife in 1790 from the Comte de Moustier. It was purchased by the Association from Mrs. Peter's descendants and stands in the Washington bedroom.

[15] The "large looking glass in the front parlour" is difficult to identify, but is probably the one in the Lewis Collection at the National Museum of American History, Smithsonian Institution, Washington, D. C.

[16] The twelve chairs and the marble top table are preserved in the Lewis Collection at the National Museum of American History, Smithsonian Institution, Washington, D. C. The two prints of "the Dead Soldier" are appraised in the "Inventory" at $45, or $22.50 each.

[17] The description in the "Inventory" is "1 Easy Chair" appraised at $10. This chair is also in the Lewis Collection at the National Museum of American History.

[18] Wine glasses and decanters are difficult things to identify documentarily, but a number of these pieces have been restored to Mount Vernon.

[19] Washington made several large purchases of china after the Revolution and during his Presidency; some of these purchases can be definitely linked with surviving Mount Vernon china. Several pieces of this "blue and white china in common use" are now at Mount Vernon. In the "Inventory" the china "in common use" may have been that which is mentioned as being "In the Closet under Franks direction" at a total appriased value of $36.85.

[20] These rings were, presumably, mourning rings like those mentioned in the General's Will. Anna Maria Washington was the daughter of George Augustine Washington and Frances Bassett.

[21] Elizabeth (Foote) Washington, the wife of Lund Washington.

[22] This word has been inserted by Mrs. Washington.

[23] Benjamin Lincoln Lear (born in 1792), the son of Tobias Lear and Mary Long, Lear's first wife.

[24] The glebe of Truro Parish (Pohick Church) seems not to have been purchased within the time limit of the provision of the will, as there is no record in the Executors' accounts of the payment of this bequest.

[25] A copy of this codicil in Mrs. Washington's handwriting is preserved in the Chicago Historical Society. Butler Washington, of King George County, Virginia, the son of John Washington, of King George County, died in 1817.

WASHINGTON GENEALOGY

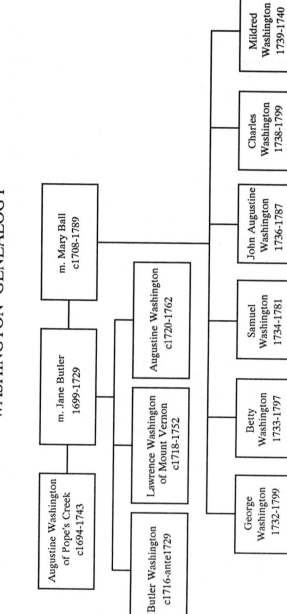

DANDRIDGE / CUSTIS GENEALOGY

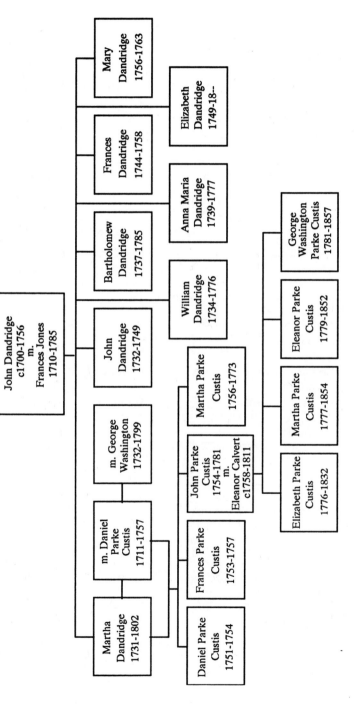

GENEALOGY

GEORGE WASHINGTON

Augustine Washington (c1694-1743) m1 Jane Butler (1699-1729) in 1715.
Their children:

Butler Washington (c1716-ante1729)

Lawrence Washington (c1718-1752) m. Ann Fairfax (c1726-1761) in
1743.
Their children:
Jane (1744-1746)
Fairfax (1746-1747)
Mildred (1748-1749)
Sarah (1750-1752)

Augustine Washington (c1720-1762) m. Anne Aylett (c1726-1773) in
c1743.
Their children:
Lawrence (c1745-ante1758)
Augustine (c1747-ante1758)
Elizabeth (1749-1814)
Ann (1752-1777)
Jane (1756-1833)
William Augustine (1757-1810)
George (c1760-c1780)

Augustine Washington m2 Mary Ball (c1708-1789) in 1731.
Their children:

George Washington (1732-1799) m. **Martha Dandridge Custis**
(1731-1802) in 1759.
No children.

Betty Washington (1733-1797) m. Fielding Lewis (1725-1781) in 1750.
Their children:
Fielding (1751-1803)
Augustine (1752-1756)
Warner (1755-1756)
George (1757-1821)
Mary (1759-1759)
Charles (1760-1775)
Samuel (1763-1764)
Betty (1765-1830)
Lawrence (1767-1839)
Robert (1769-1829)
Howell (1771-1822)

[68]

Samuel Washington (1734-1781) m1 Jane Champe (c1735-c1755) in
c1754.
Their children:
(child) c1755 - died young

Samuel Washington m2 Mildred Thornton (c1741-c1762) in c1756.
Their children:
Thornton (c1758-1787)
Tristram (c1760-ante1768)

Samuel Washington m3 Louisa Chapman (1743-c1763) in c1762.
Their children:
(child) c1763 - died infant

Samuel Washington m4 Anne Steptoe Allerton (1737-1777) in 1764.
Their children:
Ferdinand (1767-1788)
Frederick Augustus (1768-1769)
Lucinda (1769-1770)
George Steptoe (1771-1809)
Lawrence Augustine (1774-1824)
Harriott (1776-1822)

Samuel Washington m5 Susannah Perrin Holden (?-1783) in
c1778.
Their children:
John Perrin (c1780-1783)

John Augustine Washington (1736-1787) m. Hannah Bushrod
(c1738-c1800) in 1756.
Their children:
Mary (c1757-c1762)
Jane (1759-1791)
Bushrod (1762-1829)
Corbin (c1764-1799)
Augustine (c1767-c1784)
Mildred C. (c1769-c1797)

Charles Washington (1738-1799) m. Mildred Thornton (c1737-c1804)
in 1757.
Their children:
George Augustine (c1758-1793)
Frances (1763-1815)
Samuel (c1770-1831)
Mildred Gregory (1772-1804)

Mildred Washington (1739-1740)

[69]

MARTHA DANDRIDGE CUSTIS WASHINGTON

John Dandridge (c1700-1756) m. Frances Jones (1710-1785) in 1730.
Their children:

Martha Dandridge (1731-1802) m1 Daniel Parke Custis (1711-1757) in 1750.
Their children:
Daniel Parke (1751-1754)
Frances Parke (1753-1757)
John "Jacky" Parke (1754-1781) m. Eleanor Calvert (1758-1811) in 1774.
Their children:
Elizabeth Parke (1776-1832) m. Thomas Law (1756-1834) in 1796.
Martha Parke (1777-1854) m. Thomas Peter (1769-1834) in 1795.
Eleanor "Nelly" Parke (1779-1852) m. Lawrence Lewis (1767-1839) in 1799.
George Washington Parke (1781-1857) m. Mary Lee Fitzhugh (1788-1853) in 1804.
Martha "Patsy" Parke (1756-1773)

Martha Dandridge Custis m2 **George Washington** (1732-1799) in 1759.
No Children.

John Dandridge (1732-1749)

William Dandridge (1734-1776)

Bartholomew Dandridge (1737-1785) m. with issue.

Anna Maria Dandridge (1739-1777) m. with issue.

Frances Dandridge (1744-1758)

Elizabeth Dandridge (1749-18--) m. with issue.

Mary Dandridge (1756-1763)

PERSONS MENTIONED IN
GEORGE AND MARTHA WASHINGTON'S
WILLS

Birth and/or death dates of family members given when known.
Bold = in Martha Washington's will

Adams, Daniel Jenifer, 44
Alton, Jonathan, 18
Ashton, Ann Washington (1752-1777), 24
Ball, Frances Washington (1763-1815), 25
Bishop, Thomas, 18
Blackburn, Sarah Ball Haynie. *See* Haynie, Sarah Ball
Brown, Kitty [Catherine], **56**
Buchan, Earl of. *See* Erskine, David Steuart
Byrd, William, 14
Carter, Betty Lewis (1765-1830), 13, 24
Carter, Charles (c1760-1827), 13
Clinton, George, 15, 46
Coxe, Daniel, 46
Craik, James, 17
Custis, Daniel Parke (1710-1757), **57**
Custis, George Washington Parke (1781-1857), 22, 23, 25, 27, **56, 58, 61**
Dandridge, Bartholomew (1737-1785), 12, 13
Dandridge, Bartholomew (d. 1802), **55, 61**
Dandridge, Frances Lucy (d. 1808), **55**
Dandridge, John (176?-1799), 12, **60**
Dandridge, John, **59, 60**
Dandridge, Julius Burbidge (d. 1828), **61**
Dandridge, Martha Washington, **55**
Dandridge, Mary, **55**
Dandridge, Mary Burbidge (d. 1809), 12, 13
Elish (slave), **61**
Erskine, David Steuart, 16
Fairfax, Bryan (1736-1802), 17
Farrell, Roger, **61**
Franklin, Benjamin, 17
Gordon, Samuel, 14
Green, Sarah, 18
Halyburton, Martha Washington Dandridge. *See* Dandridge, Martha Washington

[71]

Hammond, Mildred Washington (1772-1804), 25
Haynie, Sally (Sarah) Ball (b. 1778), 18
Henley, Bartholomew (b. 1788), **59, 60**
Henley, Elizabeth Dandridge Aylett (b. 1749), **59**
Henley, Frances Dandridge, **55**
Henley, Samuel (1792-1825), **59, 60**
Hood, John, 14
Houckgeest, Andreas Everardus VanBraam, 57
Lafayette, Marie Joseph Paul Yves Roch Gilbert du Motier, marquis de, 17
Law, Elizabeth Parke Custis (1776-1832), 25, 57, **58**
Lear, Benjamin Lincoln (1792-1832), **58**
Lear, Frances Dandridge Henley. *See* Henley, Frances Dandridge
Lear, Tobias (1762-1816), 18, 21
Lee, William, 4
Lewis, Andrew, 44
Lewis, Betty Washington (1733-1797), 22, 24
Lewis, Eleanor Parke Custis (1779-1852), 22, 25, **57, 58**
Lewis, Fielding (1725-1781), 43
Lewis, Fielding (1751-1803), 24
Lewis, George (1757-1821), 18, 24
Lewis, Howell (1771-1822), 24
Lewis, Lawrence (1767-1839), 22, 25, 27, **55, 61**
Lewis, Robert (1769-1829), 24
Mason, Thomson, 20, 23
Maynadier, Catherine Brown. *See* Brown, Kitty [Catherine]
Mercer, _____, 42
Minge, Frances Lucy Dandridge. *See* Dandridge, Frances Lucy
Parks, Harriott Washington (1776-1822), 24, 25
Peake, Humphrey, 20
Pendleton, Philip, 10, 11
Peter, Martha Parke Custis (1777-1854), 25, 57, **59, 61**
Peter, Thomas (1769-1834), **61**
Peyton, Frances Washington Ball. *See* Ball, Frances Washington
Spence, William, **61**
Spotswood, Alexander (1746-1818), 46
Spotswood, Elizabeth Washington (1749-1814), 24
Stuart, David (1758-1815), 17
Stuart, Eleanor Calvert Custis (c1757-1811), 18, **58**
Thornton, Anna Maria Washington. *See* Washington, Anna Maria
Thornton, Jane Washington (1756-1833), 24
Thornton, Mildred. *See* Washington, Mildred Thornton

Trumbull, John, **57**

VanBraam. *See* Houckgeest, Andreas Everardus VanBraam

Walker, Ann Alton, 18

Walker, Thomas, 43

Washington, Ann. *See* Ashton, Ann Washington

Washington, Anna Maria (1788-1816), 25, **58, 60**

Washington, Augustine (c1720-1762), 24

Washington, Bushrod (1762-1829), 14, 18, 19, 22, 23, 25, 27

Washington, Butler (c1774-c1817), **61**

Washington, Charles (1738-1799), 17, 25

Washington, Charles Augustine (1791-1811), 25, 37

Washington, Corbin (c1764-1799), 25

Washington, Elizabeth. *See* Spotswood, Elizabeth Washington

Washington, Elizabeth Foote (1746-c1811), 18, **58**

Washington, George (1732-1799), **55**

Washington, George Augustine (c1758-1793), 21, 25

Washington, George Fayette (1790-1867), 21, 25

Washington, George Steptoe (1771-1809), 11, 18, 24, 27

Washington, Hannah Bushrod (c1738-c1800), 18

Washington, Hannah Fairfax (1742-1804), 18

Washington, Jane. *See* Thornton, Jane Washington

Washington, Jane Washington (1759-1791), 25

Washington, John Augustine (1736-1787), 19, 25

Washington, Lawrence (1728-c1814), 17

Washington, Lawrence Augustine (1774-1824), 11, 21, 24, 37

Washington, Martha Dandridge Custis (1731-1802), 1, 14, 15, 21, 22, 23, 25, 27,
    55

Washington, Mildred Thornton (c1739-c1804), 18

Washington, Robert (1729/30-c1800), 17

Washington, Samuel (1734-1781), 10, 11, 25

Washington, Samuel (c1770-1831), 18, 25, 27

Washington, Thornton (c1758-1787), 10, 11, 25

Washington, William Augustine (1757-1810), 14, 18, 24, 27

Willet, Marinus & wife, 45

Willie, William, 14

Willison, Mary Dandridge. *See* Dandridge, Mary

Wilson, Thomas, 17

INDEX

Bold = in Martha Washington's will

Adams, Daniel Jenifer, 44, 52

Alexandria, v, vii, xii
    Academy, 4-5, 31
    town of, vii, 4, 40
    Bank of, 5, 31, 49

Alte, Theophilus, 36

Alton, Jonathan, 18, 36

America, *see* United States

Arlington, 38, **64**

Ashbys Bent. *See* Landed
    Property, Loudoun

Ashton, Ann Washington, 24, 38

Audley, 50

Bailey, J., 36

Ball, Frances Washington, 25, 39

Ball, Mary (c1708-1789), vi, 35

Bassett, Burwell, 33

Bassett, Fanny, 35, 37

Bible, 17, 35, **57**

Bishop, Thomas, 18, 36

Boston Athenaeum, 33

Britain, 7, 19

Brown, Kitty [Catherine], **56**, **64**

Brown, William, 31

Buchan, Earl of. *See* Erskine,
    David Steuart

Burning Spring. *See* Landed
    Property, Kanhawa

Byrd, William, 14, 33

cane, xiv, 17, 34

Carter, Betty Lewis, 13, 24, 33

Carter, Charles, 13

Chattins Run. *See* Landed
    Property, Loudoun

Christ Church, 35, 39

Civil War, vii

Clinton, George, 15, 45, 52

Columbia, Bank of, 9, 49

Columbia, District of, 9

Continental Army, vii

Coxe, Daniel, 45

Craik, Dr. James, 17, 34

Crawford, William, 51, 52

Custis, Daniel Parke, 30, 31, **64**

Custis, Eleanor Parke. *See* Lewis,
    Eleanor Parke Custis

Custis, George Washington Parke,
    22, 23, 25, 27, 37, 39, **56**, **58**, **61**

Dandridge, Bartholomew
. (1737-1785), 12, 13
Dandridge, Bartholomew (d.
1802), 31, 55, 61, 62
Dandridge, Frances Lucy, 55, 62
Dandridge, John (c1700-1756), 30
Dandridge, John (176?-1799), 12,
60
Dandridge, John, 59, 60
Dandridge, Julius Burbidge (d.
1828), 61
Dandridge, Martha Washington,
55, 62
Dandridge, Mary, 55, 62
Dandridge, Mary Burbidge, 12, 13
debt, 1, 55-56, 59
Difficult Run. See Landed
Property, Loudoun County
Dismal Swamp Company, Great,
xii, 15, 33, 43, 51
distillery, 23, 38
District of Columbia, x, xii, 9
Dogue Run. See Mount Vernon
Edinburgh, Town of, 14, 33
education, 7,
National University, x, 8, 9, 32
of nephews, 11, 32, 55-60
of orphan children, 5, 31
of slaves, 3, 31
Elish (slave), 61
Erskine, David Steuart, Earl of
Buchan, 16, 34
estate,
of Bartholomew Dandridge, 12
of Benjamin Franklin, 17, 34
of George Washington, 1, 19,
24-26
of Samuel Washington, 12
executor, xii, xiii, 3, 9, 13, 24, 26,
27-28, 54, 59, 61

Falkirk, battle of, 16
Fairfax, Bryan, 17, 35, 50
Fairfax Court House, v, vii, viii
Farrell, Roger, 61
Ferry Farm, 34
Fishkill. See J. Bailey
Flexner, James Thomas, xi
Forbach, Madame de, Dowager
Duchess of DeuxPonts, 34
Fort Cumberland, 6
Franklin, Benjamin, xiv, 17, 34
Fredricksburg, 13
Freeman, Douglas Southall, xii
furnishings, 2
bed, 56-57, 58
castor, 56, 63
chair: circular, 17, 34; green
bottom, 57, 65; Martha's
chamber, 58, 65
chest, 57, 64
china: blue and white, 58, 65;
Cincinnati, 56, 63; gift of
VanBraam, 57, 64
cooler, 56, 63
curtain, 57
desk, 57, 64
garniture, 63
girandole, 56, 64
glebe, 59, 64
linen, 58
looking glass, 57, 58, 64
mantel, 63
painting, 56, 57, 63, 64
print, 57, 65
side board, 57
silver plate, 56, 63
table: dressing, 57, 64; marble,
57; shaving, 17, 34; writing,
57
tambour secretary, 17, 34
wine glass, 58, 65

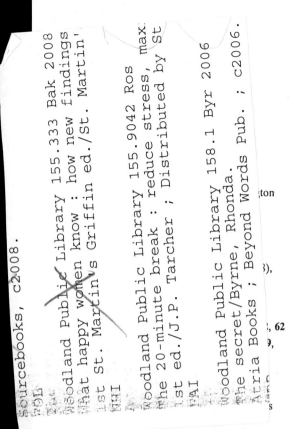

Gloucester, county of, 15, 33, 42, 51

Hampshire, 42, 50

Kanhawa, Great, 15, 33, 44

Kentucky, 46, 53

Loudoun, county of, 15, 33, 41, 50

Maryland, 44-45, 52

Mount Vernon, 19-21, 22

Nansemond, *See* Dismal Swamp Company

New York, State of, xii, 15, 33, 45, 52

Northwest Territory, xii, 45-46, 52

Ohio River, 43-44, 51

Pennsylvania, State of, 15, 33, 45, 52

Richmond, vicinity of, 14

Washington, City of, 23, 38, 46-47, 53

Winchester, 47, 53

Law, Elizabeth Parke Custis (1776-1832), 25, 39, **57, 58**

Lear, Benjamin Lincoln (1792-1832), **58, 65**

Lear, Tobias (1762-1816), vii, 18, 21, 35

Lee, Henry ("Light-Horse Harry"), 33, 51, **63**

Lee, Robert E., 32, 38

Lee, William, 4, 31

L'Enfant, Pierre-Charles, x

Lewis, Andrew, 44

Lewis, Betty Washington (1733-1797), 22, 24, 33

Lewis, Eleanor Parke Custis (1779-1852), 22, 25, 37, 39, **57, 58, 62**

Lewis, Fielding (1725-1781), 43

Lewis, Fielding (1751-1803), 24, 33

Hunting Creek, Little. *See* Mount Vernon

Jackson, A., v

James River Company, x, 10, 32, 48

Jefferson, Thomas, x, 32, 34

Lafayette, Marie Joseph Paul Yves Roch Gilbert du Motier, marquis de, 17, 35

land, xii, xiii

landed property, 26
Alexandria, xii, 1, 23, 47, 53, **55**
Bath, 47, 53
Berkeley, county of, 10-11, 42, 50
Fauquier, county of, 41, 50
Four Mile Run, 38
Fredrick, 42, 50

Lewis, George (1757-1821), 18, 24, 36

Lewis, Howell (1771-1822), 24

Lewis, Lawrence (1767-1839), 22, 25, 27, 37-38, **55**, **61**

Lewis, Robert (1769-1829), 24

Lexington, x

Liberty Hall Academy, x-xi, 10, 32

Library of Congress, viii

livestock, xii, 49

Madison, James, x, 32

Manchester, town of, 14

Mason, Thomson, 20, 23, 37

masonry, 31, 40

McClean, Archibald, 51

Mercer, George, 42, 52

Mercer, James, 30, 52

mill, 20, 23, 38

Mohawk River. *See* Landed Property, New York

Mount Vernon,
Dogue Run, 20, 23, 30, 38
estate, v, viii, ix, xi, xii, 19-21, 22, 34, 35, 36-37
history of, 30
Hunting Creek, 20, 21, 30
See Landed Property
Muddy Hole Farm, 20
River Farm, 30
Union Farm, 30

Mount Vernon Ladies' Association of the Union, v, xiv

Muddy Hole Farm. *See* Mount Vernon

National University, x, 8, 9, 32

navigation, x
James River, 6
Potomac River, 6, 26, 42

New York, xii, 15

Parks, Andrew, 33, 38, 50, 52, 53

Parks, Harriott Washington (1776-1822), 24, 25, 33, 38

Peake, Humphrey, 20, 37

Pendleton, Philip, 10, 11

Peter, Martha Parke Custis (1769-1834), 25, 39, **57**, **59**, **61**

Peter, Thomas, **61**

Philadelphia, vii

Polkinhorn, Samuel, v

Potomac Company, x, 9, 26, 32, 48

Randolph, Edmund, xiii

Revolutionary War, 4, 6, 17, 19, 21, 31, 35, 52

Robertson, Archibald, 34

Rockbridge, County of, 10

Schedule of Property, vii, xii

Shenandoah Valley, 26

Sheppard, William, 33

slaves, xi, 2, 12-13, 30, 31, 38. *See* Education

Spence, William, **61**

Spotswood, Alexander (1746-1818), 38, 46, 50

Spotswood, Elizabeth Washington (1749-1814), 24, 38

Stevens, Henry, 33

Straughan, Elizbeth Johnson Bonom, 35

Stuart, David (1758-1815), 17, 34

Stuart, Eleanor Calvert Custis (c1757-1811), 18, 34, 35, **58**

Supreme Court, xiii

tomb. *See* vault

Thornton, Jane Washington (1756-1833), 24, 28

Thornton, William, 38

[78]

Trumbull, John, **57**, **64**

Truro parish, **59**, **65**

Truxton, Thomas, **63**

United States, ix, xi, xiv, 1, 7, 29
Treasurer of, 9

VanBraam. *See* Houckgeest,
Andreas Everardus VanBraam

vault, 27, 39, 40

Vineyard Inclosure, 27

Virginia, Commonwealth of, 3, 6,
10, **62**

Walker, Ann Alton, 18

Walker, Thomas, 43

Wallace, William, xiv, 16

Washington and Lee University.
See Liberty Hall Academy

Washington, Anna Maria
(1788-1816), 25, 39, **58**, **60**, **65**

Washington, Augustine
(c1720-1762), vi, 24, 33, 37, 38

Washington, Bushrod (1762-1829),
xii, xiii, 14, 18, 19, 22, 23, 25,
27, 33, 36

Washington, Butler (c1774-c1817),
61, **65**

Washington, Charles (1738-1799),
17, 25

Washington, Charles Augustine,
25, 37

Washington, Corbin (c1764-1799),
25

Washington, Elizabeth Foote,
(1746-c1811), 18, 35, **58**, **65**

Washington, George (1732-1799),
v, vi, ix, xii, xiii, xiv, 32, 37, 39,
55
bequests of: books, 14, 33;
cane, xiv, 34; estate, 19-26,
34-37; kitchen furniture, 1-2;
monetary gift, 4, 6, 18, 31,
38; papers, 14, 33; pistol, 17,
35; ring, 18, 35; spy-glass, 17;
stock, 5, 9-10, 15, 48-89;
sword, xiv, 18-19, 36;
telescope, 17, 34.
death, vii
debt, 1
funeral, 27, 39-40
See Furnishings
General, vii
See Landed Property
nationalism, x
President, ix, xi, 32, 36
youth, 34

Washington, George Augustine
(c1758-1793), 25, 37

Washington, George Fayette
(1790-1867), 21, 25, 37

Washington, George Steptoe
(1771-1809), 11, 18, 24, 27, 36

Washington, Hannah Bushrod
(c1738-c1800), 18, 35

Washington, Hannah Fairfax
(1742-1804), 18, 35

Washington, Jane Washington, 25,
39

Washington, John Augustine
(1736-1787), 19, 25, 36

Washington, Lawrence
(1728-c1814), 37

Washington, Lawrence, 17, 34

Washington, Lawrence Augustine
(1774-1824), 11, 21, 24, 27

Washington, Lund, 35

Washington, Martha Dandridge
Custis, vii, ix, xi, xiii, 1, 14, 15,
21, 22, 27, 31, **55**
bequests of: books, **57**;
monetary gift, **58**; ring, **58**,
65; stock, **58**, **59**; wine, **56**,
58, **63**.
See Furnishings
debt, **55-56**, **59**

Washington the Man and Monument, v

Washington, Mildred Thornton (c1739-c1804), 18, 35

Washington, Robert (1729/1730-c1800), 17, 34

Washington, Samuel (1734-1781), 10, 11, 25

Washington, Samuel (c1770-1831), 18, 25, 27, 36

Washington, Thornton (c1758-1787), 10, 11, 25

Washington, William Augustine (1757-1810), 14, 18, 24, 27, 33, 36

water mark, vi, xiii

Whitehead, William B., 51

will, George's, v-xiv
  display of, viii
  importance of, xii
  layout of, vi, xiii
  ownership of, vii
  purpose of, ix
  publication of, v
  restoration of, viii
  selection of, vii

will, Martha's, viii, **62**

Willet, Marinus & wife, 45

Willie, William, 14

Wilson, Thomas, 17, 35

Woodlawn, 36